Yōkoso *(Welcome)!*

Kyoto that has more than 1200 years of history is

the most interesting city in Japan.

Would you step out of your sightseeing bus and

fly around Kyoto?

KYOTO The Greatest Travel Tips
英語で歩く京都

Contents
目次

Culture
◆文化

Lodging
◆泊まる

Directory
◆便利帳

Transport
◆交通

Map Section
◆地図

World Cultural Heritage and more with Rakubus

洛バスで世界文化遺産＋α

洛バスは、京都市内の世界文化遺産などの観光地をめぐる急行バス。路線は100・101・102の3路線あり、リボン柄デザインの車体がとても目を引く。運賃は220円均一で、乗車カード（P97参照）を利用すれば乗り降り自由だ。

大徳寺
Daitoku-ji

金閣寺
Kinkaku-ji

北野天満宮
Kitano-tenman-gū

京都御所
Kyoto Imperial palace

二条城
Nijō-jō

KYOTO TOWER

京都駅
Kyoto station

Rakubus is an express bus service that takes passengers to tourist spots such as World Cultural Heritage sites within the city of Kyoto. There are 3 routes numbered 100, 101 and 102, and the ribbon-style design of the buses is very eye-catching. Fares are a standard ¥220. If you take advantage of a bus card (see p.97) you can use any Rakubus freely. The routes intersect at places including Ginkaku-ji-michi, Horikawa Imadegawa intersection and Kitaōji bus terminal, and transfers are also possible.

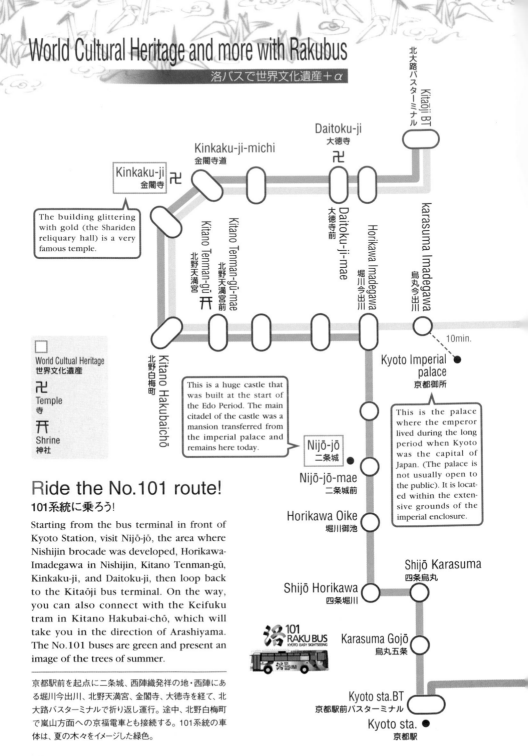

Ride the No.101 route!
101系統に乗ろう!

Starting from the bus terminal in front of Kyoto Station, visit Nijō-jō, the area where Nishijin brocade was developed, Horikawa-Imadegawa in Nishijin, Kitano Tenman-gū, Kinkaku-ji, and Daitoku-ji, then loop back to the Kitaōji bus terminal. On the way, you can also connect with the Keifuku tram in Kitano Hakubai-chō, which will take you in the direction of Arashiyama. The No.101 buses are green and present an image of the trees of summer.

京都駅前を起点に二条城、西陣織発祥の地・西陣にある堀川今出川、北野天満宮、金閣寺、大徳寺を経て、北大路バスターミナルで折り返し運行。途中、北野白梅町で嵐山方面への京福電車とも接続する。101系統の車体は、夏の木々をイメージした緑色。

Ride the No.102 route!
102系統に乗ろう!

The No.102 route runs east-west through the city. From Ginkaku-ji, the bus proceeds to Imadegawa-dōri, Kyoto Imperial palace, Kitano Tenman-gū, Kinkaku-ji and Daitoku-ji, and then loops back to the Kitaōji bus terminal. On the way, the bus converges with the route of the No.101 bus. The No.102 buses are yellow and present an image of the ginkgo trees of autumn.

市内を東西に走る路線。銀閣寺から今出川通りを西へ進み、京都御所、北野天満宮、金閣寺、大徳寺を経て、北大路バスターミナルで折り返し運行。途中、101系統のバスともルートを併走する。102系統の車体は、秋のイチョウをイメージした黄色。

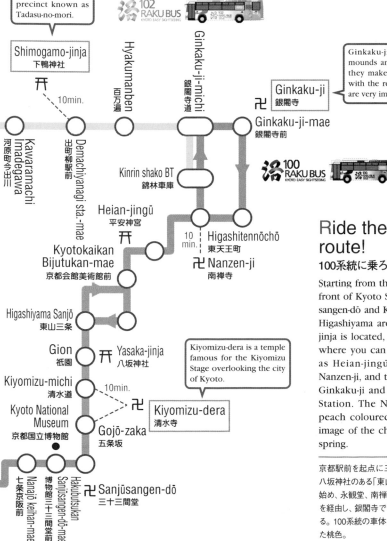

Shimogamo-jinja is one of the oldest shrines in Kyoto, with the main hall of the shrine standing in a huge shrine precinct known as Tadasu-no-mori.

Ginkaku-ji, the two sand mounds and the landscape they make in combination with the rest of the garden are very impressive.

Kiyomizu-dera is a temple famous for the Kiyomizu Stage overlooking the city of Kyoto.

102 RAKU BUS KYOTO EASY SIGHTSEEING

100 RAKU BUS KYOTO EASY SIGHTSEEING

Shimogamo-jinja
下鴨神社

10min.

Hyakumanben
百万遍

Ginkaku-ji-michi
銀閣寺道

Ginkaku-ji
銀閣寺

Ginkaku-ji-mae
銀閣寺前

Kawaramachi Imadegawa
河原町今出川

Demachiyanagi sta.-mae
出町柳駅前

Kinrin shako BT
錦林車庫

Heian-jingū
平安神宮

Kyotokaikan Bijutukan-mae
京都会館美術館前

10min.

Higashitennōchō
東天王町

Nanzen-ji
南禅寺

Higashiyama Sanjō
東山三条

Gion
祇園

Yasaka-jinja
八坂神社

Kiyomizu-michi
清水道

10min.

Kiyomizu-dera
清水寺

Kyoto National Museum
京都国立博物館

Gojō-zaka
五条坂

Nanajō keihan-mae
七条京阪前

Hakubutsukan Sanjūsangen-dō-mae
博物館三十三間堂前

Sanjūsangen-dō
三十三間堂

Ride the No.100 route!
100系統に乗ろう!

Starting from the bus terminal in front of Kyoto Station, visit Sanjū sangen-dō and Kiyomizu-dera, the Higashiyama area where Yasaka-jinja is located, the Okazaki area where you can find places such as Heian-jingū, Eikan-dō and Nanzen-ji, and then loop back to Ginkaku-ji and return to Kyoto Station. The No.100 buses are peach coloured and present an image of the cherry blossoms of spring.

京都駅前を起点に三十三間堂や清水寺、八坂神社のある「東山エリア」、平安神宮を始め、永観堂、南禅寺のある「岡崎エリア」を経由し、銀閣寺で折り返して京都駅に戻る。100系統の車体は、春の桜をイメージした桃色。

Visit places early in the morning

Kiyomizu-dera 清水寺
MAP P107F4 東山区清水1丁目294
10 min walk from the Gojō-zaka or Kiyomizu-michi city bus stop
6:00〜18:00 (Times differ during periods of evening admission)
Entrance fee ¥300

13:30 pm

There can be too many people in Kyoto in the sightseeing seasons of spring and autumn and you can sometimes get weary of it. Because of that, we recommend making early morning visits to places. From the stage of Kiyomizu-dera, with its view out over the city, you can see a glorious view of Kyoto illuminated by the early morning sun as it rises over Higashiyama.

春秋の観光シーズンの京都は人が多くてうんざりしてしまうこともある。そこでお勧めなのが、早朝拝観。京都市街が眺望できる清水寺の舞台からは、東山から昇る朝日が街を照らす絶景が見られる。

6:30 am

Let's visit temples and shrines

神社や寺院で参拝しよう

Sanpai is the Japanese term for a visit to a shrine or temple to worship the Shintō or Buddhist deities. Worshipping means to make a wish to a god or to Buddha. The way people worship is different at shrines and temples so you need to take care.

参拝とは、神社や寺院に行って神仏を拝む行為のこと。神社と寺院とでは参拝の仕方が違うので、注意が必要だ。

The general way to worship

一般的な参拝方法

1 Wash your hands and rinse your mouth at the *chōzuya* to purify your body.

手水舎（ちょうずや）で手を洗い、口をすすぎ、身を清める。

2 Put a money offering into the offertory.

賽銭を賽銭箱に入れる。

3 If there is a bell hanging down, ring it.

鈴や銅鑼が下がっていれば鳴らす。

Money offerings
賽銭

These were originally money given as a thank you when a prayer had been realized. When people visit a shrine or temple to worship, they make offerings as compensation for the wish and to show their appreciation. No amount is set. If their wish is for marriage ties, some people decide the amount to give with a play on words - make a *go-en* (¥5) wish for *go-en* (marriage)!

社寺に参拝する時に、祈願や感謝の代償として供える。金額は決まっておらず、縁結びなら「ご縁（5円）」と語呂合わせで決めることもある。

In the case of a shrine
神社の場合

4 Bow deeply twice, clap your hands twice, and pray with the hands together. Then, bow deeply once more.

2回深くお辞儀をして2回の拍手を打ち、手を合わせたまま拝む。そのあと、もう一度1回深くお辞儀をする。

PAN PAN

Shrines
神社

A shrine is a religious institution created based on affiliation with Shintō. A lot of gods are worshipped. There is usually woodland known as Chinju-no-mori around the shrine.

神道信仰に基づく宗教施設。やおよろずの神様が祀られている。まわりには鎮守の杜と呼ばれる森林があるのが一般的。

In the case of a temple
寺院の場合

4 Bow deeply once and pray with the hands together.
※ Do not clap your hands

1回深くお辞儀をし、手を合わせて拝む。
※拍手を打ってはダメ

Temples
寺院

A temple is a building for the practice of Buddhist religious rituals. Buddhism is the religion that began with Shakyamuni. Buddhism is divided into many sects.

釈迦を開祖とする仏教に基づく宗教施設。多くの宗派に分かれている。

11

Famous free cherry blossom and autumn colour sites

無料で楽しめる桜、紅葉の名所

MAP P109D4
上京区京都御苑3
1 min walk from Imadegawa Station on the Karasuma subway line

Kyoto Gyoen
京都御苑

There are about 30 big weeping cherry trees with drooping branches planted in the north-west of the Gyoen. These cherry trees are the earliest to blossom in the Gyoen, with their buds starting to open from late March. Because there are many cherry trees planted in this expansive park and the periods they flower in differ depending on their type, you can enjoy the cherry blossoms in the Gyoen for about a month.

御苑北西部には枝垂れ桜の大木が約30本ある。これらは御苑で一番早く3月下旬にはほころび始める。広い苑内にはたくさんの桜があり、種類によって開花時期が異なることから、約1ヵ月間楽しめる。

Maruyama Park
円山公園

MAP P107F3
東山区円山町463
5 min walk from the Gion city bus stop

Kyoto City established Maruyama Park in 1886. The famous weeping cherry tree with fabulous drooping branches is the second generation to be planted here. The original tree lived for 220 years and died in 1947. Subsequently, seeds were taken from the original tree and the tree cultivated from it transplanted to the park.

1886年に京都市が開設した公園。見事な枝ぶりで有名な枝垂れ桜は現在2代目。初代は樹齢220年で1947年に枯死した。その後、初代より種子を採って育成された桜が植栽された。

12

Many tourists visit Kyoto to see cherry blossoms in the spring and autumn colours in the autumn. The reason for the popularity of such visits is because the beautiful buildings of the shrines and temples combine with the scenery of the cherry blossoms or autumn colours. That allows visitors to enjoy even more emotive scenes. Here we introduce some recommended spots where you can savour such beautiful scenery free of charge.

京都には春の桜、秋の紅葉を見に多くの人が訪れる。人気の理由は、美しい社寺の建物と桜や紅葉の景色が相まって、さらに情緒ある眺めが楽しめるからだ。

The Sanmon Gate of Nanzen-ji
南禅寺の三門

The Sanmon Gate of Nanzen-ji is counted as one of the "three gates of Japan". The Sanmon Gate was constructed in 1295 and despite being burnt down, was rebuilt in the Edo Period. In autumn, the spectacular view provided by the gate is further enhanced by the addition of the changing colours of the autumn trees.

※ The temple grounds may be visited without charge, but a fee is required to visit areas such as the Hōjō Garden and the top of the Sanmon Gate building.

日本三大門のひとつに数えられる南禅寺の三門。1295年に創建され、一度は焼失したものの江戸時代に再建された。
※方丈庭園、三門楼上などは拝観料が必要

MAP P102D3
左京区南禅寺福地町
7 min walk from Keage Station on the Tōzai subway line

MAP P105E4
東山区本町15丁目778
10 min walk from Tōfukuji Station on the JR Nara line

Tōfuku-ji
東福寺

Every autumn, visitors can enjoy the scenery given by the changing colours of about 2000 trees spread throughout the Sengyokukan ravine, which cuts through the center of the temple grounds. It is possible to savour freely the appearance of the Tsūten Bridge that hangs above the Sengyokukan ravine and the autumn colours of the trees that spread out below it from the Ga'un Bridge in front of the temple grounds.

※ A fee is required to visit areas such as the Tsūten Bridge, the Kaizan-dō and the Hōjō Garden at Tōfuku-ji.

境内中央の渓谷には約2000本もの紅葉が広がる。そこにかかる通天橋とその下に広がる紅葉を手前の臥雲橋から自由に眺められる。
※通天橋・開山堂、方丈庭園などは拝観料が必要

13

Which amulet do you like?

Kamigamo-jinja air travel safety amulet
上賀茂神社　航空安全お守り

The god worshipped at Kamigamo-jinja protects the sky. It is said that Kamotaketsume-no-Mikoto, the grandfather of this god, guided the journey of Emperor Jinmu, the first emperor of Japan, from the sky. This amulet, which is used to pray for safety during travel, was created from that folklore tradition.

上賀茂神社の祭神は天空を守護する神で、その祖父神は、かつて神武天皇の旅路を空から先導したといわれている。その伝承からできた旅の安全を祈願するお守り。

Kamigamo-jinja 上賀茂神社
MAP　P102C2
北区上賀茂本山339

Nashi-no-ki-jinja sickness and convalescence amulet
梨木神社　病気平癒お守り

Somei Water, one of the "three famous waters" of Kyoto springs into the purifying water basins found within the grounds of Nashi-no-ki-jinja. If you drink some of the famous water and wear an amulet, you need not worry about becoming sick.

京都三名水のひとつ「染井（そめい）の水」が、境内の手水舎に湧き出る梨木神社。名水を飲み、お守りを身につけたら病気になる心配もないとか。

Nashi-no-ki-jinja 梨木神社
MAP　P109D4
上京区寺町通広小路上ル染殿町680

Jishu-jinja marriage amulet
地主神社　縁結びお守り

Ōkuninushi-no-Mikoto, the god of marriage, is worshipped at Jishu-jinja. All sorts of amulets are lined up for prayers involving matchmaking and love.

縁結びの神様である大国主命を祀る地主神社。良縁・恋愛祈願のお守りが各種揃う。

Jishu-jinja 地主神社
MAP　P107F4
東山区清水１丁目317

Amulets include a benefit from a Shintō god or from Buddha and are supposed to have various effects such as helping wishes come true or repelling evil things. People buy amulets at shrine or temple and then either wear them on their bodies or put them in a specified place. Choose an amulet that you like according to its shape and effect.

お守りには、神や仏からのご利益が込められ、願い事をきいたり悪いものを退けてくれたりとさまざまな効力があるとされる。形や効力で好きなものを選べる。

Rokkaku-dō monk's amulet
六角堂　お坊さんのお守り

The Buddhist Saint Shinran is the model for this amulet. He visited Rokkaku-dō from Mt. Hiei every day for a period of 100 days for ascetic training. The Rokkaku-dō monk's amulet is supposed to be effective for academic achievement and fitness.

修行のために比叡山から六角堂まで100日間通い続けたという親鸞上人がモデル。学業成就・体力増進に効力があるとされる。

Rokkakudō 六角堂
MAP　P106C2
中京区六角通東洞院西入ル堂之前町248

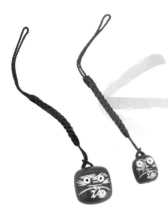

Imamiya-jinja Daruma amulet
今宮神社　だるまお守り

When you point the face of this Daruma amulet downwards, the eyes pop out, signifying the emergence of a bud, and thus new growth and flowering. This amulet is popular among students preparing for tests and finding employment, among other things.

「め」（芽）が出るようにと、だるまの顔を下に向けると目がピョコっと飛び出してくる。受験生や就職祝いなどに人気。

Imamiya-jinja 今宮神社
MAP　P102C2
北区紫野今宮町21

Nonomiya-jinja Ise-jingū vestal virgin amulet
野宮神社　斎宮お守り

The models for this Nonomiya-jinja amulet are the vestal virgins who serve at Ise-jingū Shintō's holiest and most important site. Nonomiya-jinja was the place where the vestal virgins purify themselves before going to serve at Ise-jingū. Because it has been passed down that purified women will be accorded a good match, this amulet is supposed to be effective for easy childbirth and success in love.

モデルは伊勢神宮に仕えた女性・斎宮。ここは斎宮が伊勢神宮に仕える前に身を清めた場所。清らかな女性に良縁が授かると伝わることから、安産や恋愛成就に効力があるとされる。

Nonomiya-jinja 野宮神社
MAP　P110B3
右京区嵯峨野宮町1

★★★★★ ★ ★ ★ ★ ★ ★
★ A Written Oracle No. 1
★ ★ ★ ★ ★ ★ ★ ★ ★ ★

運　勢　大　吉

災害自から去り福徳集まり
誠に平地を行くが如く追手
の風に舟の進むが如く目上
の人の助をうけて喜事があ
ります　信心怠らず心直く

わがおもう
港も近く
なりにけり
ふくや
追手の
かぜの
まにく
行い正しくなさい

願望	金銭其他万事心任です安心油断大敵	
待人	たよりなし　来る	
失物	出る　人手に渡らず	
旅行	行先利徳あり	
商売	売物買物損はなし	
学問	安心して勉学せよ	
相場	好機です	

争事	勝つが控えて吉	
恋愛	この人となら幸福あり	
転居	いそがぬ方が吉	
出産	安し　母子とも大吉	
病気	精神の安定第一	
縁談	首尾よし思わず早く調う安心せよ	

The Japanese-English omikuji of Nishiki Tenman-gū

錦天満宮の和英文みくじ

The *omikuji* at Nishiki Tenman-gū are written in Japanese and English. You can get one from the *karakuri* lion dancing machine inside the shrine precincts.

和文と英文で占い結果が記されたおみくじ。境内のからくり機械（獅子舞）で引くことができる。

裏には…

How to draw an omikuji

There are various ways to draw an *omikuji*. These include dropping a stick from a small hole in a cylindrical box containing lots of thin sticks and receiving the *omikuji* with the number written on the stick. At other places, you choose a folded-up *omikuji* from a box and at others you buy one from an automatic machine, etc.

People draw *omikuji* when they visit a shrine or temple in order to read their fortune. A long time ago, *omikuji* were used to read the intentions of the gods. The *omikuji* includes a phrase expressing your general fortune such as excellent, good, reasonable, fair or evil fortune, as well as advice on individual topics such as the overall state of your fortune, your health, things you are searching for and people you are waiting for.

古くは、神の意思をうかがうために用いたおみくじ。「大吉・吉・中吉・小吉・凶」などの運勢を表す語句のほか、健康、探し物、待ち人などの個別の項目についてのアドバイスが記されている。

11

My old harbor. I'm getting close to you. My friendly wind, help me sail on fast.

Your Fortune	Excellent

Evils are gone, good luck has come. Just like you sail before the wind, someone who is older than you will help you. You'll be happy if you are faithful and honest.

■ **wish** : Leave everything to others, not to speak of money matter.
■ **expected visitor** : He[or she] will come without writing to you.
■ **missing thing** : You can find it. There's no fear that it might pass to others.
■ **travel** : You'll be satisfied wherever you go.
■ **business** : You can buy or sell any time. You'll never lose.
■ **study** : No problem. Keep studying.
■ **speculation** : It's high time.
■ **game and match** : You'll win, but go steadily.
■ **love** : You'll be happy with her(him).
■ **removal** : You had better not make haste.
■ **childbirth** : Easy. Both a mother and a baby will be well.
■ **illness** : Firstly keep your mind steady.
■ **marriage proposal** : It will go well sooner than you expect.

Take it easy.

How to draw a karakuri (lion dancing machine) omikuji at Nishiki Tenman-gū
錦天満宮のからくりおみくじ（獅子舞）の引き方

1 Throw your money (￥200) and then press the Japanese/ English *omikuji* button.
金額分（￥200）の硬貨を投入し、和英文みくじのボタンを押す。

2 The *karakuri* lion dancing machine draws an *omikuji* for you.
からくり仕掛けの獅子舞がおみくじを引いてくれる。

3 Take the *omikuji* from the pick-up place and accept its contents seriously.
受け取り口からおみくじを取り出し、その内容を真摯に受け止める。

4 If you want to form a connection with the gods or Buddha, tie your *omikuji* to the branch of a tree or a rope inside the shrine precincts.
※ If you tie your *omikuji* to a tree at a shrine or temple recklessly, you can damage a plant or disrupt the scenery. Make sure to tie your *omikuji* at a place designated for doing so.
神や仏との縁を結びたいなら、境内の木の枝や縄などにおみくじを結びつけて。おみくじは、必ず指定された場所に結ぼう。

Nishiki Tenman-gū 錦天満宮
MAP　P107D3
中京区新京極通四条上ル中之町537
5 min walk from Hankyū Kawaramachi Station
8：00～21：00

17

Let's pray for a good match

❶ Writing a wish on a *katashiro*.

形代に願い事を書く。

The relationship breaking and making stone of Yasui-Konpira-gū
安井金比羅宮の縁切り縁結び碑（いし）

This shrine has a giant stone 1.5m high and 3m wide. It is said that the power of the gods flows into the round hole on the top side of the stone. So many pieces of *katashiro* paper (paper notes containing wishes that substitute for the people who make them) with wishes written on them have been stuck on the stone, that the stone itself can barely be seen!

高さ1.5m、幅3ｍの巨大な石で、神様の力が石の下方の円形の穴に注がれていると言われている。願い事を書いた形代（かたしろ＝自分の身代わりとなるよう願いを込める紙のおふだ）が碑が見えないほど貼られている。

❷ Pass through the hole in the stone from front to back to break off a bad relationship, and pass through from back to front to make a good one. Lastly, stick the *katashiro* on the stone and make your wish.

碑の表から裏へ穴を通って悪縁を切り、裏から表へ通って良縁を結ぶ。最後に形代を碑に貼って願い事を祈る。

Yasui-Konpira-gū
安井金比羅宮
MAP　P107E3
東山区東大路松原上ル下弁天町70
3 min walk from the Higashiyama Yasui city bus stop
Katashiro ￥100

The mysterious power that binds people with others is called "en". There is a concept in Buddhism called "engi", which says that all things in the world are mutually interrelated. Buddhism values "en". In Kyoto too, many visitors go to shrines and temples that are said to be good for prayers for a good match in love.

人と人とを結ぶ、不思議な力のことを「縁」という。仏教では世界のあらゆるものはお互いに関わり合っているという「縁起」の考え方があり、「縁」を大切にする。京都でも良縁祈願にご利益があると言われる社寺には多くの参拝客が訪れる。

The love fortune telling stone of Jishu-jinja
地主神社の恋占いの石

2 guardian stones stand about 10m apart. The story is that if you walk from one stone to the other with your eyes shut and reach your target, you will find love. It is said that if you manage to reach your target without mishap in one attempt, you will be quick to succeed in love. However, the more attempts you have, the longer it will take you to succeed.

10メートルほど離れて立つ2つの守護石。片方の石から反対側の石に目を閉じて歩き、たどり着けると恋がかなうと伝わる。一度で無事たどり着ければ恋の成就も早く、回数を重ねるほど恋の成就も遅れると言われている。

Jishu-jinja 地主神社
MAP　P107F4
東山区清水1丁目317
15 min walk from the Gojō-zaka or Kiyomizu-michi city bus stop
9：00〜17：00
¥300(Entry to Jishu-jinja requires Kiyomizu-dera entry fee)

19

Let's appreciate Buddhist images

Bosatsu
菩薩(ぼさつ)

This is a Buddhist in training who is trying to become enlightened and thus a Buddha. A Bosatsu takes on the roles of guiding and helping people.

悟りを開き、仏になろうと励む修行者。人々を導き、救済する役割も担う。

Nyorai
如来(にょらい)

Nyorai means an enlightened person. This is the highest state of existence in Buddhism, in other words, Buddha.

悟りを開いた人を意味する。仏教上の最高の状態にある存在。

How many arms does a Senju Kannon have?
千手観音(せんじゅかんのん)の手は何本?

A Senju Kannon is a kind of Bosatsu. There are actually some that have 1000(=千) arms depicted, but they generally have 42. The reason the rest are omitted is supposed to be that there are 25 Buddhist worlds and they are saved by the 40 arms remaining after excluding the 2 hands clasped in prayer in front of the chest (40×25 = 1000).

千手観音は菩薩のひとつ。実際に千本の手を表現したものもあるが、42本のものが一般的。なぜなら、仏教では世界が25に分かれており、胸の前で合掌する2本の手を除いた40本の手でそれぞれ25の世界を救う(「40×25=1000」)とされるから。

Buddha images are statues or pictures of Buddha, the object of faith in the Buddhist religion. In many cases, the term Buddhist image refers to statues that are made of a variety of materials including metal, stone and wood. They are not used just as objects of faith and veneration, but have also drawn attention in recent years as works of art due to the beauty of their forms.

仏像とは仏の姿を彫刻や絵画で表現した像のこと。多くの場合は彫刻を指し、材質は金属、石、木などさまざま。信仰や礼拝の対象としてだけでなく、造形の美しさから美術品としても注目されている。

Myō-ō
明王(みょうおう)

A Myō-ō guides people who have received the life of Nyorai to Buddhist teaching to make them believe.

如来の命を受けて、教えに従わない人々を帰依させようと強制的に教えに導く。

Tenbu
天部(てんぶ)

Tenbu gods guard against the enemies of Buddhist teaching, who try to disturb Nyorai, Bosatsu, and Myō-ō. Many Tenbu are thought to be gods from ancient Indian mythology prior to the establishment of Buddhism.

如来、菩薩、明王たちを邪魔する仏敵から守る神。その多くは、仏教成立以前の古代インドの神々と考えられる。

So many prayers

Kyoto's many *torii* shrine gates, images of arhats and Daruma and other religious icons are the highlights of a sightseeing trip. All of them are donated by worshippers for the sake of prayers and their fulfillment. Sense the prayers and wishes of these people from the many statues and other icons gathered in Kyoto.

見る者を圧巻するたくさんの鳥居、羅漢、だるま…。そのひとつひとつは、祈願のためや祈願成就のお礼のために参拝者から納められたもの。集まった数々のものから人々の祈りを感じとろう。

The Senbon Torii of Fushimi Inari Taisha
伏見稲荷大社の千本鳥居

The reason so many *torii* have been built at this great shrine in Fushimi is because they have been donated in order to have prayers realized or in gratitude for the realization of prayers. At present, approximately 5000 *torii* shrine gates line the mountainside approach to the shrine.

鳥居がたくさん建っているのは、願い事が「通る」ようにあるいは「通った」お礼に鳥居が次々に奉納されたから。現在は約5千基の鳥居が山の参道全体に並ぶ。

Fushimi Inari Taisha
伏見稲荷大社
MAP　P103C4
伏見区深草薮之内町68
1 min walk from JR Inari Station

The arhats of Otaginenbutsu-ji

愛宕念仏寺の羅漢

As many as 1200 figures of arhats stand in the temple grounds. Carved and dedicated by worshippers, they are figures of the monks and arhats who have become disciples of Buddha and communicated Buddhist teaching. Each face is different and it is said that you can a face that looks like you if you search hard enough.

境内に並ぶ1200体もの羅漢は、参拝者自らが彫って奉納したもの。釈迦の弟子となり仏教を伝えた僧・羅漢たち。それぞれ表情が違い、自分に似た顔が必ずあるといわれる。

Otaginenbutsu-ji 愛宕念仏寺
MAP P102A3
右京区嵯峨鳥居本深谷町2-5
1 min walk from the Otagi-deramae Kyoto bus stop 8：00～17：00 Entrance fee ¥300

Hōrin-ji 法輪寺
MAP P111C3 上京区下立売通御前西入ル
4 min walk from JR Enmachi Station
9：00～16：30 Entrance fee ¥300

The Daruma of Hōrin-ji

法輪寺のだるま

Approximately 8000 figurines and Daruma dolls portraying Saint Daruma sitting in his famous Zazen position are enshrined in the Daruma Hall within the grounds of the temple. These Darumas have been dedicated by people from across the country praying for the realization of their wishes.

境内の達磨堂には、本尊である達磨大師の坐禅姿を模した置物・だるまが約8000体安置されている。これらのだるまは願い事の成就を祈って全国の人々より奉納されたもの。

23

Are dragons good or bad?

龍はいいやつ？わるいやつ？

The dragon is an imaginary creature. Dragon imagery varies widely depending on the country and the stories they appear in, and they are depicted as almost godlike creatures as well as beasts to be feared. In the west, dragons are often depicted as fierce monsters, but in the Buddhist culture of the east, dragons are revered as dragon gods who aid in the spread of the teachings of Buddha. You can see many decorations using the dragons as motifs in Japanese temples. Some of these include the *Unryū-zu* dragon pictures of Tenryūji and Nanzen-ji.

想像上の生き物・龍。西洋では獰猛な怪獣として描かれることが多いが、東洋の仏教文化では仏の教えを助ける龍神としてあがめられる。日本の寺院では天龍寺や南禅寺の雲龍図など、龍をモチーフとした装飾が多く見られる。

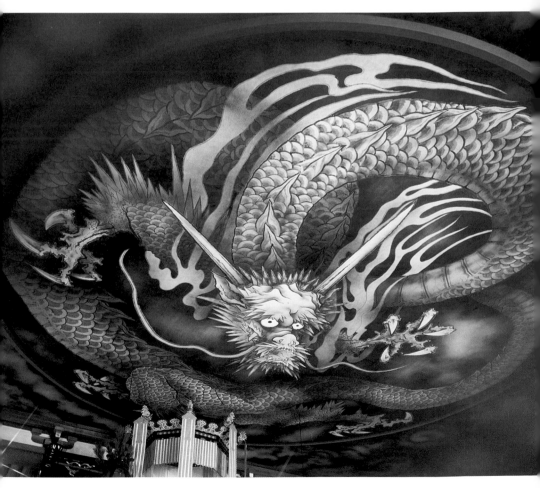

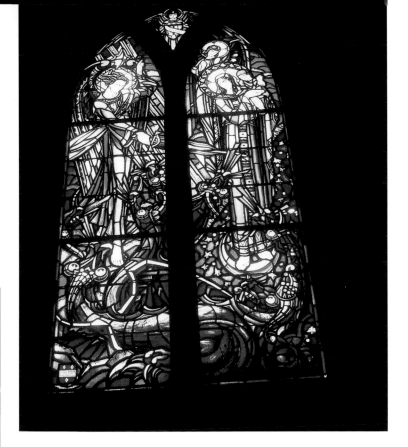

A dragon acting as a guardian deity

守護神としての龍

Unryū-zu on the ceiling of the Dharma hall at Tenryū-ji painted by Kayama Matazō. (Usually closed to the public)

加山又造画伯によって描かれた天龍寺・法堂（はっとう）の天井の雲龍図（通常は非公開）。

A Dharma hall is a building used by resident priests to explain Buddhist teachings. By depicting a dragon that rules over water, this picture incorporates a wish for the prevention of fires. It also includes the meaning of rain (Buddhist teaching) falling from heaven.

法堂は住職が仏法を説くための建物。水を司る龍を天井に描くことで、火災を防ぐようにという祈りが込められている。また、法の雨（仏法の教え）を降らすという意味も込められている。

Dragon being slain by St. Michael

大天使ミカエルに退治される龍

This is a stained glass window at a monastery on Mont St Michel, a small island off the western coast of France. The dragon is depicted as a symbol of evil.

フランス西海岸に浮かぶ小島、モン・サン・ミッシェルの修道院にあるステンドグラス。龍は悪の象徴として描かれる。

Tenryū-ji 天龍寺
MAP　P110B3
右京区嵯峨天龍寺芒ノ馬場町68
5 min walk from Arashiyama Station on the Keifuku railway Arashiyama line
8：30〜17：30（〜17：00 October 21 to March 20）
Garden entry fee ￥500（Entry to the Dharma Hall requires a separate ￥500 fee）

Sacred mountain - Mt. Kurama

神聖なる山―鞍馬山

Kurama area is at the deep mountain in about an hour from Kyoto Station. In Japan, mountains are considered to be sacred places. In the past, Kurama was also used as a place for ascetic training. Shrines and temples such as Kurama-dera, Yuki-jinja and Kibune-jinja are dotted around the area so try wandering around.

日本では、山は神聖な場所だと考えられ、かつて鞍馬は修行場所でもあった。山中には鞍馬寺や由岐神社、貴船神社などの寺社が点在するのでゆっくり歩いて回ろう。

Kurama-dera 鞍馬寺
MAP　P102C1
左京区鞍馬本町1074
To Niō Gate 1min walk from Eizan Kurama Station
9:00〜16:30
Entrance fee ¥200

A mountain range to watch in front of a main temple　本殿前から見る山並

Kurama hot spring
くらま温泉

Visit a hot spring inn after wandering through the mountains of Kurama. The waters of the Kurama hot spring are said to be effective for neuralgia, rheumatism, diabetes, beautiful skin and back pain, among other things. In an open-air bath, you can bathe while viewing the scenery of the mountains, which change appearance with each passing season.

鞍馬温泉の湯は、神経痛やリュウマチ、糖尿病、美肌、腰痛などに効能があるとされる。露天風呂では、季節ごとに表情を変える山々を目にしながら入浴できる。

Kurama hot spring
MAP　P102C1
左京区鞍馬本町520
10 min walk from Hiei Kurama Station
(there is a free bus from the station)
10:00～21:00
Bathing charges　¥1100～

An open-air hot spring bath
露天風呂

What is the Kurama Tengu?
鞍馬天狗とは?

A number of anecdotes and folklore legends remain in Kurama. Among them the story that the Kurama Tengu lives in the area is famous. The Tengu is a creature of folklore that is supposed to have a big nose on a red face, and to wear tall wooden sandals in addition to a *kimono* and a tasseled surplice. The Kurama Tengu flies through the air and to create strong winds using a fan made from the fatsia shrub.

鞍馬には、逸話や伝承がいくつも残り、なかでも鞍馬天狗が住むというものは有名。天狗は伝説上の生き物で、空を飛んだり、ヤツデのうちわで強力な風を起こしたりする。

Kyoto's sounds

In Kyoto, you can hear a lot of unique sounds - sounds that evoke feelings of the seasons or that create an atmosphere distinctively Japanese. At the same time that they have beauty to the ear, these sounds are used practically.

京都では季節を感じさせたり、和の雰囲気を盛り上げてくれたりする独特の音色を聞くことができる。それらは音色としての美しさを持つのと同時に実用性も兼ねている。

Suikinkutsu
水琴窟

A *suikinkutsu* is a device born from the culture of tea and makes a strange sound "Pōn" like the plucking of a *koto*. At a tea party, many people use a washbasin (=*chōzubachi*) to wash and purify themselves prior to the tea ceremony and the *suikinkutsu* is thought to have been developed to prevent the intrusion of water into the garden.

「ポーン」と琴のような不思議な音色がする、茶の文化から生まれた装置。お茶会でたくさんの人が手水鉢を使うので、庭が水浸しになるのを防ぐために考えられた排水装置。

The structure of a Suikinkutsu 仕組み

A pot with a small hole in its base is buried upside down in the garden beneath the *chōzubachi* basin. Water that leaks from the basin gradually accumulates in the upside down pot. Whenever a drop of water falls from above onto the surface of the water in the pot below, a sound is emitted.

手水鉢の下に、底に小さな穴を空けた甕を逆さまに埋める。鉢から漏れ入る水がどんどん甕の中に溜まり、水面にしずくが落ちるたびに甕の中で共鳴して音を発する。

Taizō-in, sub-temple at Myōshin-ji
妙心寺塔頭 退蔵院
MAP　P111B3
右京区花園妙心寺町35
8 min walk from JR Hanazono Station
9:00～17:00
Entrance fee ￥500

Shishiodoshi
ししおどし

"Kapōn"- a *shishiodoshi* makes a pleasant tapping sound that penetrates through the ear. This sound brings the Japanese atmosphere to the gardens and restaurants where it is found. Originally, the *shishiodoshi* was used as an equipment to threaten animals that damage crop fields.

「かぽーん」と耳を突きぬける心地よい音。庭園や料亭などで雰囲気を盛り上げてくれるししおどしは、元々、田畑を荒らす動物を威嚇するために使われていた音の装置。

The structure of a Shishiodoshi 仕組み

Water pours into a bamboo cane open only at one end. At the other end, a stone is placed as a tapping stand. After a little while, the bamboo can no longer support the weight of the water and tips up. When the water rushes out and the bamboo returns to its original position, it hits the tapping stand and makes sounds.

片方の口が開いている竹筒に水を注ぎ込み、反対側には石などのたたき台を置く。しばらくすると、水の重さに耐えかねた竹が傾いて水をはき出し、元の傾きに戻った際にたたき台をたたいて音を発する。

Nightingale floors
うぐいす張り廊下

Floors make the sound, "Kekyo-Kekyo" just like the birdcall of a nightingale. You can hear this kind of floor at places such as Nijō-jō. It is said that these singing floors were made accidentally and another that they were made to prevent people from being intruded because the corridor sounds whenever somebody walked along.

「キュッ、キュッ」と、うぐいすの鳴き声に似た音を発する廊下。二条城などで耳にすることができる。偶然にできたという説や、廊下を歩くたびに音が鳴るため侵入者対策だという説がある。

The structure of a nightingale floor 仕組み

The joist that supports the floor panels and floors are fastened using a metal part known as an eye brace and nails. Whenever somebody walks along the corridor, the eye brace and the nails rub against each other and emit a noise.

廊下の床板と床板を支える根太という板は、目かすがいという金属と釘で固定されている。人が廊下を歩く度、目かすがいと釘が擦れ合って音を発する。

Nijō-jō 二条城
MAP P106B1
中京区二条堀川西入ル二条城町541
1 min walk from subway Tōzai line Nijō-jō-mae Station
8:45〜17:00(admission until 16:00)
Entrance fee ￥600

The deep and interesting world of Zen gardens

奥深い禅庭の世界

In general, Japanese gardens have garden stones and plants arranged around a central pond to create a scene that can be appreciated throughout the four seasons. However, the culture of "wabi-sabi" spread from the Muromachi Period onwards, and a garden style known as karesansui also developed. A karesansui-style garden expresses natural mountain and river scenes using stones and sand, and without using sources of water such as ponds. You can see many such gardens at Zen temples in particular, in forms suitable for Zazen and other forms of meditation.

日本庭園は一般的に、池を中心に庭石や草木を配置し四季を通して鑑賞できる景色を造る。「侘び・寂び」の文化が広まった室町時代以降、池などの水を使わず石や砂などで山や川といった自然の風景を表現する枯山水という庭園様式が発達。瞑想や坐禅にふさわしい造形として、特に禅宗寺院で多く見られる。

Mountain

Bridge

Water

Small stones carpeting the south garden are used to represent the surface of water, with the pattern on the surface expressing the flow of the water.

南庭に敷き詰められた小石は水面を見立てたもので、表面の紋様は水の流れを表現する。

Following the death of Hideyoshi Toyotomi, his wife Nene spent the remainder of her days at Entokuin, a sub-temple of Kōdai-ji. In 1605, a garden was transferred from Fushimi Castle, where Nene and Hideyoshi shared deep memories, to become the north garden of Entokuin. Mountains and waterfalls are represented with combinations of stones, and a bridge across a pond is represented with stones crossing over a depression in the ground.

豊臣秀吉の没後、その妻・ねねが晩年を過ごした高台寺の塔頭・圓徳院。その北庭は、秀吉との思い出が深い伏見城にあった庭を1605年に移したもの。石組みで山や滝を、くぼみに渡した石で池にかかる橋を表している。

Entoku-in, sub-temple at Kōdai-ji
高台寺塔頭 圓徳院
MAP　P107F3
東山区高台寺下河原町530
5 min walk from Higashiyama Yasui city bus stop
10:00～17:00 (Reception open until 16:30)
※ Times differ during evening admission periods
Entrance fee ¥500

Aiming at Buddhahood

悟りの境地を目指して

The enlightenment of Buddhism is to cast away doubts and awaken to the truth of the world. Enlightenment is the ultimate purpose of Buddhism and believers undertake various training in order to achieve it.
Zazen is one of the basic types of training found in the Zen branch of Buddhism. Practitioners of Zazen pursue mental concentration by sitting in a straightened posture. You may be able to get this image by sitting quietly in front of the famous Window of Enlightenment called "Satori-no-mado" at Genkō-an. If you want to study in earnest, there are also Zazen meetings held in groups.

仏教での悟りとは、迷いを捨て世界の真理に目覚めること。究極の目的であり、そのためにさまざまな修行が行われる。中でも坐禅は、禅宗の基本的な修行法のひとつ。

姿勢を正して座り、精神統一を行う。源光庵の「悟りの窓」の前に座ればこのイメージがつかめるかもしれない。本格的に学びたいなら、坐禅会もある。

Genkō-an 源光庵
MAP P102B2
北区鷹峯北鷹峯町47
☎075-492-1858
1 min walk from the Takagamine Genkō-an-mae
bus stop
9：00〜17：00
Entrance fee ￥400

Zazen meetings are held on the first Sunday of each month.
(There is no meeting in August. There is also sometimes no
meeting in January or December either.) Booking is required
(Tel: 075-492-1858). Note that meetings are not held in front
of the Window of Enlightenment and Window of Doubt.
※ 坐禅会は第1日曜日（8月は休会。1、12月は休会の場
合もある）に行われる（要予約）。ただし、「悟りの窓」
「迷いの窓」の前では行われない。

The round window on the left is known as the Window of Enlightenment, which represents the heart of Zen and the universe. The square window on the right is known as the Window of Doubt called "Mayoi-no-mado" and represents all of the troubles of human beings.

In Buddhism, the round shapes are symbols of Buddhahood, and many round-shaped expressions are used in the *mandala* pictures that depict the Buddhist world.

左側の丸窓は「悟りの窓」と呼ばれ、禅の心と宇宙を表す。右側の角窓は「迷いの窓」と呼ばれ、人間のあらゆる苦しみを表す。仏教における円は悟りの境地の象徴であり、仏教の世界観を表した絵画「曼荼羅（まんだら）」にも円形の表現が多数用いられる。四季折々の窓の外の風景も併せて味わいたい。

Creating memories at shrines and temples

Have a goshuin made
御朱印をしてもらおう

A *goshuin* is a red stamp you receive at a shrine or temple as a memento of your visit. The term *goshuin* also includes having information such as the name of the temple and the date you visited written in your notebook in ink (this information is printed in some cases). Usually, for a donation of ¥200 to ¥500 (an offering to the temple), you can have the stamp, etc, entered in a special notebook (*goshuin-chō*) sold at shrines and temples.

参拝の記念として社寺で押してもらう印のこと。社寺名や参拝日などの墨書(印刷物の場合もある)も含めて御朱印と呼ばれる。

通常は200円〜500円ほどの金銭(初穂料・御布施)を納め、社寺などで売られている御朱印帳にしてもらう。

Try copying a sutra by hand
写経をしてみよう

In Buddhism, *shakyō* means to copy a sutra by hand. In former ages, when printing technology had not yet been developed, all temples copied sutras in order to spread the teachings of Buddhism. Nowadays, sutras are often copied out in order to obtain merit. Usually, you trace the sutra by putting the copybook over the paper. You can take the paper that you wrote home with you.

仏教において経典を書写すること。
印刷技術が発展していなかった時
代には仏法を広めるために各寺で
行われていた。今では、功徳を得
るために写経をすることが多い。お
手本の上に紙をのせて上からな
ぞるのが一般的。書いたものは
持ち帰れる。

Tenryū-ji 天龍寺
MAP P110B3
右京区嵯峨天龍寺芒ノ馬場町68
5 min walk from Arashiyama Station on the Keifuku railway
Arashiyama line
8：30〜17：30 (8：30〜17：00 October 21 to March 20)
Sutra copying roll ￥1000 ※ Bookings required
(Entry to the temple requires a separate fee)

Shōjin vegetarian cuisine with deep connections to temples

お寺とつながりの深い精進料理

Seigen-in,sub-temple at Ryōan-ji 龍安寺塔頭 西源院
MAP　P111A2
右京区竜安寺御陵下町13
1 min walk from the Ryōan-ji-mae city bus stop
10：00～17：00
Budged：￥3300

Shōjin cuisine was developed for Buddhist monks, who are forbidden to destroy life. Shōjin cuisine is prepared using vegetables and beans. Cooking methods such as boiling vegetables in water and removing bitter tastes have also had an effect on food prepared in general households and restaurants. You can try shōjin cuisine such as *yudōfu* and *shira-ae* at Seigen-in, a sub-temple at Ryōan-ji.

精進料理とは、殺生が禁じられている仏教の僧侶のために発展した、野菜や豆類を調理した料理のこと。野菜の水煮やあく抜きなどの調理法は、一般家庭や飲食店で作られる料理にも影響を与えた。龍安寺の塔頭・西源院では、湯豆腐や白和えなどの精進料理がいただける。

I want to meet geiko and maiko

芸妓さんと舞妓さんに会いたい

Even today, entertainment areas where *geiko* and *maiko* practice their arts flourish in Kyoto. *Geiko* are not prostitutes, but rather learn dancing and how to play musical instruments like *koto* to entertain their customers with artistic skills. *Maiko* are women undertaking training to become *geiko* and have a flashy appearance with false bottom sandals accompanying a limp *obi* sash and long sleeved *kimono*.

京都には今も芸妓と舞妓が活躍する花街が栄える。芸妓は遊女とは違い、踊りや琴などの楽器を習い、芸能で座を盛り上げる。舞妓はその修行中の身で、華やかな格好をする。

Gion Corner
ギオンコーナー

Parlors where visitors can directly meet a *maiko* or *geiko* turn away first-time customers. However, at Gion Corner in the Yasaka Kaikan, you can experience the company of these rather difficult-to-find women at close quarters. Every night, *maiko* hold a show to perform Kyoto dancing. Apart from dancing, tea ceremonies, *koto*, flower arrangement, court music and dancing, comic drama and puppet drama are also held, you can enjoy Japan's traditional arts fully. There is also a tea ceremony experience class. Performances take place from 19pm and 20pm every night.

舞妓さんや芸妓さんと直接対面できるお座敷は一見さんお断り」。しかし、中々お目にかかれない彼女たちを弥栄会館のギオンコーナーでは、間近で見ることができる。毎夜、ここでは舞妓さんが京舞を披露する公演が開催。他にも茶道、琴、華道、雅楽、狂言、文楽が披露されるので、日本の伝統芸能を堪能することができる。茶道体験教室もある。公演は毎夜19時と20時から。

Glon Corner ギオンコーナ
MAP P107E3
東山区祇園花見小路四条下ル
10 min walk from Keihan Shijō Station
Performance times：3/1 to 11/30 - 19：00～、20：00～
(12/1 to 2/28 - 19：00～ on Fri, Sat, Sun, and public holidays)
Closed:8/16, the end and the begining of the year
Admission fee ¥3150

Kyōmai 京舞

Koto 琴

Kadō 華道

Kyōgen 狂言

Gagaku 雅楽

Time that you may see geiko and maiko
この時間帯に会えるかも？
17：30～18：00

Spots where geiko and maiko appear
出現スポット
Hanamikōji, Gion Shirakawa, Miyagawa-chō, Ponto-chō, Kamishichiken
花見小路・祇園白川・宮川町・先斗町・上七軒

Try dressing you in a Japanese kimono

着物を着てみよう

1 Tying the hair　　髪を結う

If your hair is about 10cm in length, you can set a *maiko* hairstyle using a half-wig. Because the half-wigs are used for making the most of your natural hair, they join with the hairline beautifully and naturally.

髪は10cm程長さがあれば、半かつらで結うことができる。地毛を使うので生え際も美しい。

2 Makeup　　メイク

Your face is painted white and eyelashes drawn on. A deep red lipstick is also applied. Vermilion is used for eyeliner to give very glamorous eyes.

白塗りをして、まゆを描いて。唇には真っ赤な紅がさされる。アイラインも朱色。

3 Finish　　完成

Once you are dressed in your chosen *kimono*, you will look just like a *maiko*! You can have your photograph taken with your own camera of course, or you can have it taken by a professional photographer. You can also walk around nearby.

選んだ着物を着付けてもらう。持ち込みのカメラでの撮影はもちろん、プロのカメラマンの撮影も可能。店の近くの散策も可能。

Maika
舞香
MAP P107E3
東山区四条下ル宮川筋4丁目297
☎075-551-1661
5 min walk from Hankyū Shijō Kawaramachi Station
9：00～19：00
Maiko dressing plan ￥6500～
Booking required　要予約
http://www.maica.net/form.htm

There is a studio in Kyoto that you can transform yourself into an adorable *maiko*. Have your face painted white and your hair tied up high before being dressed in a *kimono*. There is also a plan that allows you to go out sightseeing in Kyoto in your new guise. You may even be mistaken for a real *maiko*!

京都にはあこがれの舞妓さんに変身できるスタジオがある。白塗りに髪を高く結い、着物を着付けてもらう。そのまま観光できるプランもある。

Kimono rental is recommended for people who want to try looking like a traditional Japanese woman casually. If you rent a *kimono*, the staff at the shop will dress you in it. Choose the *kimono* you like from among a wide array of colours and patterns such as red, blue, purple and yellow.

気軽に楽しむなら着物レンタルがお勧め。着物を借りて、お店の方が着付けてくれる。さまざまな色や柄の中から、好きなものを選ぼう。

Nishijin Textile Center
西陣織会館
MAP P108B3
上京区堀川通今出川南下ル
☎075-451-9231
13 min walk from Imadegawa Station on the Karasuma subway line
9:00～17:00
Booking required by the previous day　要予約
Kimono rental ￥3600

Kyoto Kimono Passport
京都きものパスポート

Enjoy sightseeing in Kyoto dressed in a *kimono* and with a Kyoto Kimono Passport. If you carry this passport, you will be able to receive various benefits and perks such as benefits at shrines and temples, and discounts and mementoes at art galleries, hotels and shops.
※In every autumn when this passport is issued, this passport is available at a tourist information center in Kyoto city.

着物姿で京都きものパスポートを提示すれば、社寺、美術館、博物館、店などでさまざまな優待や特典を受けることができる。
※パスポートが発行される秋に、京都市内の観光案内所で入手できる。
http://www.kimono-passport.jp/

I want to meet ninja and samurai!

Ninja
忍者

Ninja were spies who worked secretly behind the scenes from the Kamakura Period to the Edo Period. They learned various special disciplines. Wearing *ninja* clothing and masks of dark blue and other colours, these spies used *ninja* weapons such as the *ninja* star projectile and the *kunai* knife. In addition, the *ninja* also used the martial art of *ninjutsu* to hide in water to deceive their enemies.

忍者とは特殊訓練を積み、鎌倉時代から江戸時代に暗躍したスパイ。忍び装束や覆面を身にまとい、飛び道具の手裏剣やくないなどの忍具を使う。また、水中に隠れて敵の目を欺くといった忍術も使う。

You can meet *ninja* and *samurai* at Toei Movie Land in Uzumasa! Streets of the Edo Period are recreated in the theme park established alongside the movie studios. On the open sets and in the studios, visitors can see vigorous performances by actors dressed up as *ninja* and *samurai*.

太秦映画村で、忍者や侍に会うことができる！ 撮影所に併設されたテーマパークで、江戸時代の街並みを再現。オープンセットやスタジオでは、忍者や侍に扮した役者の迫力ある演技が見られる。

Samurai
侍

The *samurai* were the people who controlled the politics of Japan from the Kamakura Period to the Edo Period. The way of the *samurai* spread from the Edo Period onwards, whereby a warrior had to behave with a noble spirit. The ethos of the way of the *samurai*, which valued honour more than money, can be seen in the saying that "A *samurai*, even when starving, acts as if his stomach is full" meaning that a *samurai* must put on a brave display even in the face of adversity. (The literal translation of this saying is that a *samurai* should use a toothpick to make it look just like he has eaten even if he is too poor to be able to eat!)

Toei Movie Land　東映太秦映画村
MAP　P102B3
右京区太秦東蜂ケ岡町10
5 min walk from Uzumasa Keryū-ji Station on the Keifuku line
9:00〜17:00
(9:30〜16:00 December 〜 February)
Entrance fee ¥2200

江戸時代以降、「武士は気高くふるまうべし」という武士道が広まる。金銭よりも名誉を重んじる武士道の風潮は、「武士は食わねど高楊枝」（貧しくて食事ができなくても、まるで食べたかのように楊枝を使う）ということわざからも見てとれる。

Take a dip at a sentō bathhouse

Examples of poor bath etiquette

入浴NG例

To avoid entering either the men's bath or the women's bath by mistake, look at the curtains above each entrance.(男湯 = Men, 女湯 = Women)

男湯、女湯と書かれたのれんを見て入ろう。間違えないように!

Don't dive straight into the bath. Wash with hot water and clean your body before entering the bath. Take off clothes and the underwear without fail! Don't wear the swimsuit either.

すぐさま浴槽に飛び込んではいけない。お湯を浴び、体を洗ってから浴槽に入ろう。

Don't enter your towel in the bathtub. Wash your body in the washing space outside the bathtub.

タオルを浴槽に浸けてはいけない。体は外の洗い場で洗う。

Don't enter the changing room still wet from their bath. Use your towel to dry yourself off in the bath area.

体が濡れたまま脱衣室に出てはいけない。浴場内でタオルを使って体をふこう。

Visitors to a public bathhouse pay a charge to take a bath. Separated into male and female sections, visitors remove their clothes in the changing rooms and enter their respective bathing areas. In the bathing areas, there are the actual baths and washing areas. The number of cozy little old-style bathhouses is decreasing with the passing years, and in recent times, the number of large-scale bathing entertainment facilities has increased. They are called "Super Sentō", which combine various types of facilities such as eating and drinking spaces with bathing areas.

料金を払って入浴する公衆浴場。男女に分かれて脱衣所で服を脱ぎ、それぞれの浴場に入る。浴場は浴槽と洗い場に分かれる。こぢんまりとした昔ながらの銭湯は年々軒数を減らし、近年では飲食スペースなどの各種施設を併設した「スーパー銭湯」という大型の入浴娯楽施設が増えている。

Funaoka Onsen
船岡温泉

Funaoka Onsen is a bathhouse that retains some of its original character as a gourmet inn built in 1923. While visitors are also able to feel the length of the establishment's history, the bathing areas, which were renovated in 1998, are spacious and clean. The changing and bathing areas are classed as national Tangible Cultural Properties.

Curtains displaying the name of the bathhouse and the gender are often hung at the entrance to a bathhouse.

銭湯の入り口には、店名や性別が記されたのれんが掛けられていることが多い。

1923年に建てられた料理旅館の面影を残す銭湯。歴史の長さを感じさせつつも、1998年に改装された浴場は広くてきれい。脱衣場と浴場は国の有形文化財。

Pictures of horse racing at Kamigamo-jinja, etc, are carved into the wooden panels of the changing rooms at the Funaoka Onsen. There are also reliefs of Ushiwakamaru, a legendary twelfth-century Japanese warrior hero, undertaking ascetic training on Mt. Kurama, and Tengu.

脱衣場の欄間には上賀茂神社の競馬（くらべうま）の様子などが彫られる。天井には鞍馬山で修行した牛若丸と天狗のレリーフも。

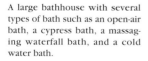

A large bathhouse with several types of bath such as an open-air bath, a cypress bath, a massaging waterfall bath, and a cold water bath.

露天風呂のほか、檜風呂、打たせ湯、水風呂など複数の浴槽が並ぶ広い浴場。

Pictures have been painted on the walls of the bath areas and elaborately designed tiles are also used.

浴場には壁に絵が描かれていたり、凝った模様のタイルが使われていたりする。

Funaoka Onsen 船岡温泉
MAP　P108A2
北区紫野南舟岡町82-1
5 min walk from the Senbon Kurama-guchi city bus stop
15:00～25:00（8:00～25:00 Sun and public holidays）
Bathing charges ￥390

How to enjoy Kaiseki tea-ceremony cuisine

懐石料理の楽しみ方

Shitsurae decoration and cuisine that evokes the seasons

季節を感じるしつらえ・料理

A Japanese restaurant is not simply a place for eating food. Whether it is the food, of course, the flowers and hanging scrolls that adorn the rooms or the dishes upon which the food is served, everything is calculated with awareness of the seasons for the entertainment of the visitor. Enjoy that thoughtfulness along with the food.

料亭はただ料理を食べる場所ではない。料理はもちろん、部屋に飾られた花やかけ軸、盛りつける器とどれをとっても季節を意識し、客をもてなすために計算しつくされている。食事と一緒に、その心遣いを楽しもう。

What is Kaiseki tea-ceremony cuisine?
懐石料理とは

Originally, *Kaiseki* tea-ceremony cuisine was presented as a meal prior to drinking tea at a tea ceremony. *Kaiseki* tea-ceremony cuisine currently available at Japanese restaurants has taken on that style. *Kaiseki* cuisine has firmly inherited the spirit of the tea ceremony that values entertainment and *shitsurae* decoration. On the other hand, there are also aspects of contemporary *Kaiseki* tea-ceremony cuisine that have origins in the culinary tradition of *Honzen* cuisine (also known as *Kaiseki* cuisine, but written with different characters and developed for drinking sake rather than tea), which was presented to the warrior warlords of former times.

元は、茶会でお茶を飲む前の腹ごしらえとして出されていた。現在、料亭で食べられる懐石料理はもてなし・しつらえを大切にする茶道の精神をしっかりと受け継いでいる。一方、大名に出された本膳料理（会席料理）を起源とするものもある。

Discover the flow of Kaiseki tea-ceremony cuisine!
懐石料理の流れを知ろう!

The order and menu of *Kaiseki* tea-ceremony cuisine differs according to the restaurant, so the introduction here is restricted to the general flow of *Kaiseki* tea-ceremony cuisine.

店によって出てくる順番や内容はそれぞれだが、ここで一般的な懐石料理の流れを押さえておこう。

先付・八寸

The first Hassun dish (on the day preparations begin for the New Year) uses a utensil shaped like an arrow, in connection with the saying "Time flies like an arrow".

1 Sakizuke and Hassun hors d'oeuvres

A restaurant will serve something made from ingredients that characterize the season as *Sakizuke*. In addition, *Hassun* is a dish that most forcefully evokes feelings of the season with its garnishments. These dishes provide seasonal vegetables and give meaning to the utensils.

先付けは季節を象徴する食材を使ったものが出る。また八寸は盛りつけで最も季節感を意識した一皿。

向付

If you don't have any problems eating *wasabi*, try placing some on *sashimi* rather than mixing it with soy sauce.

2 Mukōzuke, a dish for eating while drinking sake

Sashimi is often served for the *Mukōzuke* course, but there are also times when items such as a dish of raw fish or vegetables seasoned with vinegar or a pickled dish will be served. With *sashimi*, the lightly seasoned fish is often arranged at the front so the diner should eat the dish in order from the front backwards.

刺身が出されることが多いが、なますや酢の物などの場合もある。刺身は淡泊な味の魚が手前に盛られていることが多いので、手前から順に食べていくといい。

腕物

If the lid is difficult to open, apply a little force using your left hand on the side of the bowl. The lid will open simply if you try to make the bowl bow down a little.

3 Wanmono, a soup dish

Inside the beautiful glazed bowl is a clear broth along with a filling such as fish. This is the star of *Kaiseki* tea-ceremony cuisine. Because this dish is presented in a form covered by a lid, you will enjoy the fragrance drifting upwards alongside the steam as you open it up.

懐石料理の花形。フタをした状態で出されるので、開けた時に湯気とともに立ち上る香りを楽しもう。

煮物

Kyoto *nimono* is made using light flavouring, allowing you to enjoy the vivid colours of the vegetables. Try to feel the flavour of the broth and ingredients.

4 Nimono, a boiled dish

Kindled vegetables are the general *nimono* dish served. Kindling is a method used to take advantage of the flavour of the raw ingredients. The different types of ingredients are boiled separately and arranged in a single dish to serve.

炊き合わせが一般的。炊き合わせとは素材の持ち味を生かすための手法で、異なる種類の素材をそれぞれ別の鍋で煮てひとつの器に盛りつけたもの。

焼物

The photograph shows a dish of grilled yellow-tail. If you make a request in advance, the restaurant should be able to serve a meat dish in place of fish.

5 Yakimono, a grilled dish

This is almost always grilled fish. If you communicate a desire for volume in advance, there are also times when a fried dish such as *tempura* will be served.

焼き魚がほとんど。ボリュームがほしいことを前もって伝えれば、天ぷらなどの揚げ物が出ることもある。

蒸し物

When you have finished eating, close the lid and place the spoon at the back of the dish. This is the sign that you have finished eating the dish.

6 Mushimono, a steamed dish

When the steamed dish is served, the restaurant staff will tell you that rice is the next course. If you have had sufficient food and drink, ask for them to bring out the rice, but if you would like to enjoy some more, reply that you would like a little more time.

蒸し物が出されたら「後はごはんになります」と声をかけてくれるので、料理やお酒が十分なら「お願いします」、まだお酒や食事を楽しみたいなら、「もう少し後で」と答えよう。

ご飯・
香の物・
留腕

The photograph shows radish rice incorporating *daikon* radish, but you may also be served with simple boiled white rice. Tomewan dish is miso soup.

7 Rice, Kōnomono pickles, Tomewan soup

Tomewan soup incorporates the significance that all that remains is dessert. The alcoholic drinks are removed and hot tea served in their place. Savor the afterglow of the cuisine that you have been served to this point.

留椀には「残るは水物のみ」という意味がある。お酒は下げられ、かわりに熱いお茶が出てくる。

水物

When Mizumono dessert dish is served, Kaiseki tea-ceremony cuisine is complete. After you have finished eating and the time is right, settle your bill in the room.

8 Mizumono, a dessert dish

In accordance with its name, which suggest something watery, a dish will be served such as seasonal fruit or jelly that is juicy and fresh. Unlike desserts from culinary traditions such as that of France, most *Mizumono* dessert dishes are simple affairs that take advantage of fresh ingredients.

瑞々しくさっぱりとした季節の果物やゼリーなどが出てくる。素材を生かしたシンプルなものがほとんど。

Japanese dining etiquette
和食のマナー

In a Japanese restaurant, try to appreciate the consideration of the *shitsurae* decoration and entertainment style and handle the dishes served with care. In particular, the utensils used can be of high artistic value. So be careful when using them, including holding them with both hands so that they are not damaged.

料亭では、しつらえやもてなし方といった心遣いに感謝し、出されたものを丁寧に扱うようにしよう。特に、器は美術的価値の高いものが使われることもあるので、傷をつけないよう両手で扱うなど注意を。

If the chopsticks are laid out in rolled paper, it is considered attractive to extract them by holding the rolled paper with the left hand and pulling the chopsticks out downwards with the right hand without breaking the paper.

箸が巻紙で留められている場合は紙を破らず、左手で巻紙を押さえ右手で奥の箸を下に引き出すように取り出すと美しい。

Utensils of a size to be held in the hand should be picked up for eating. When enjoying soup, it is OK to sip directly from the bowl.

手に収まるサイズの器は持ち上げて食べる。汁を味わうときは直接器に口をつけてOK。

Drop any liquid or drops attached to a lid into the bowl. It looks more attractive if you try to hold the lid still and upright over the right-hand side of the bowl with your hand for a little while.

フタについた滴は器の中に落とす。椀の右端あたりで立てた状態でしばらく手を止めるようにすると、美しく見える。

Because drops of water attach to the lids used, turn them upside down and place them outside of the tray. By placing lids like this, it prevents the table getting wet.

器のフタは水滴がついているので、うら返して折敷の外へ。

When you have finished eating from a utensil with a lid, return the lid. At such times, you should try to line up the picture on the lid and the picture on the bowl. Putting the lid back on the bowl is a sign that you have finished eating.

フタのある器は食べ終わったらフタを閉める。この時、フタと器の絵が合うようにするといい。フタをすることで、食べ終わったというサインになる。

Kyōyamato
京大和

Removed from the bustle of the streets, Kyōyamato is in a location allowing a panoramic view of Higashiyama, where the changes of the four seasons are displayed in rich colour. The landscape seen from the viewing platform in the garden was used in the movie "Sayuri".

町の喧騒から離れ、四季の変化が色濃く表れる東山を一望できるロケーション。庭の展望台からの景色は映画「SAYURI」にも使われた。

Kyōyamato 京大和
MAP P107F4
東山区高台寺桝屋町359
☎075-525-1555 ※Bookings required
5 min walk from the Higashiyama Yasui city bus stop
11:30〜13:30LO, 17:00〜19:00LO Budged:¥8400〜 (lunch) ¥26250〜 (dinner)
http://www.kyoyamato.com/English/english.html

Try eating a Kyotoesque lunch
京都らしいランチを食べよう

Teoke bentō
手をけ弁当

The *Teoke bentō* can be eaten at a Kyoto restaurant opened in 1899. A *teoke* was originally a piece of equipment that its user put a liquid such as water into and carried around. At this restaurant, food made using seasonal ingredients such as flavoured egg-roll and grilled fish is crammed into a *teoke*. This idea made sophisticated Kyoto cuisine into something more accessible.

1899年創業の京料理店で食べられる「手をけ弁当」。手桶とは本来水などの液体を入れ、持ち運ぶための道具。この店では、手桶の中にだし巻き卵や焼き魚など旬の素材を使った料理を彩りよくつめている。このアイデアが高級な京料理をより身近なものにした。

Teoke bentō

Rokusei 六盛
MAP　P107F1
左京区岡崎西天王町71
10 min walk from Higashiyama Station on the Tōzai subway line
11：30〜15：00, 17：00〜21：00 (11：30〜21：00 Sat, Sun and public holidays)
Teoke bentō ¥3150 (service charge not included)

Kyoto cuisine has a high-class image of dining in a sophisticated Japanese restaurant, but there are also things that can be eaten for affordable prices. Carefully made lunches that although reasonably priced, have a firm grasp on the basics of Kyoto cuisine demonstrate the high level of food in Kyoto.

京料理は、料亭で食べるという高級なイメージがあるが、手頃な値段で食べられるものもある。リーズナブルだけど、京料理の基本をきちんと抑え、丁寧に作られたランチは京都の料理のレベルの高さを教えてくれる。

Saiku-zushi set

Saiku zushi
細工寿司

This is the *sushi* of Kyoto and is nibbled on while watching a *kabuki* or *Nō* performance, or eaten at a glamorous setting such as a tea party. Consequently, this style of *sushi* has a gorgeous appearance and calls for flavouring that remains delicious even over time and allows the *sushi* to be eaten without dipping in soy sauce (it may be eaten after dipping in soy sauce however). *Saiku-zushi* is made with the technique of *sushi* professionals cultivated by a demand that could only exist in Kyoto. *Saiku-zushi* may take some time to be served as it takes time to prepare. If you can speak Japanese, it is better to make a reservation by telephone.

歌舞伎や能を見ながらつまんだり、茶会などの華やかな席で食べられた京都の寿司。見た目が華やかで、時間が経ってもおいしく、江戸前寿司のように醤油に浸けなくても食べられる味つけが

求められた（浸けて食べてもよい）。細工寿司は京都ならではの需要が育んだ寿司職人の技なのだ。作るのに手間がかかるため出てくるまでに時間がかかることもある。

Chidori-tei 千登利亭
MAP P107E3
東山区団栗通大和大路西入ル六軒町203
3 min walk from Keihan Shijō Station
11：00～20：00LO
Saiku-zushi set ￥1500～2000

51

Savour some tōfu

Yudōfu

湯豆腐

Yudōfu is a cuisine in which *tōfu* is placed in hot water flavoured lightly with something such as kelp and eaten while it is kept hot in the pot. Because the soup has almost no flavour in itself, the *tōfu* is eaten after dipping in a soy sauce based marinade along with finely-chopped cibols and a spice such as *shichi mi*, a chili pepper mix of seven flavours. *Yudōfu* is often eaten in winter.

湯豆腐とは、豆腐を昆布などで出汁を取ったお湯の中に入れ、鍋の中であたためながら食べる料理。出汁自体には味がほとんどついていないので、ねぎや七味などの薬味とともに、醤油ベースのつけだれに浸けて食べる。冬によく食べられる。

Okutan, Nanzen-ji branch
奥丹 南禅寺店
MAP　P102D3
左京区南禅寺福地町86-30
10 min walk from Keage Station on the Tōzai subway line
11：00〜16：00LO, 〜16：30LO on Sat, Sun, public holidays
Yudōfu set ¥3,150

You can enjoy *yudōfu* while gazing at a splendid Japanese garden.
素敵な日本庭園を眺めながら、湯豆腐を味わえる。

About 80% of *tōfu* is water. It is said that what makes the *tōfu* of Kyoto so delicious is that the city is blessed with underground reserves of soft water perfect for making *tōfu*. Also, *tōfu* was valued highly as vegetarian fare in many temples and various *tōfu* cuisines have been developed.

豆腐の約80%は水。京都の豆腐がおいしいのは、豆腐に適した軟水の地下水に恵まれているからとされる。また、多くのお寺で、精進料理として豆腐が重宝されたため、さまざまな豆腐料理が生まれた。

Tōfu snacks 豆腐のおやつ

Soy milk rare cheesecake
豆乳レアチーズケーキ

At this cafe in Kyoto, you can find rare cheesecake made using lots of homemade soy milk. Healthier than ordinary cheesecake, this soy milk variety is very popular among females. It has a fresh flavour, but is very creamy to the taste. Black sesame is used for the pastry on the bottom.

自家製の豆乳をたっぷりと使ったレアチーズケーキ。普通のチーズケーキよりもヘルシーで、女性に大人気。さっぱりとした味わいだが、口当たりはとてもクリーミー。下の生地は黒ごまを使っている。

TO-FU CAFE FUJINO
MAP P111C2
上京区今小路御前通西入ル
2min walk from Kitano-Tenman-gū bus stop
10:30～20:00
Soy milk rare cheesecake and chiffon cake set ¥580
(¥945 with drink)

You can enjoy light meals and desserts made using *tōfu* and soy milk.
自家製の豆腐や豆乳を使った軽食やデザートが楽しめるカフェ。

Soy milk doughnuts
豆乳ドーナツ

Doughnuts made with soy milk have a light, fluffy texture. In order to bring out the flavour of the soy milk, no extra flavours are added and sweetness is also quite reduced. Eat these doughnuts soon after they have been fried. They are also reasonably priced.

豆乳入りのドーナツは、ふわふわと軽い食感。豆乳の味を引き立てるため、余計な味はいっさいつけず、甘さもかなり控えめ。揚げたてをすぐに食べよう。価格もリーズナブル。

Konna Mon Ja こんなもんじゃ
MAP P66
中京区錦小路堺町通角
5 min walk from Hankyū Karasuma Station
10:00～22:00(Doughnuts can be bought until 19:00)
¥150 (8 doughnuts)

Inside Nishiki Market, the market representative of Kyoto
京都を代表する市場「錦市場」の中にある。

What is the way of tea?

Commonly referred to as the 'tea ceremony' in the West, the way of tea or Chado is a way of entertaining guests with tea. The four principles of the way of tea are Harmony, Respect, Purity and Tranquility. These were written by Sen no Rikyū who lived during the Azuchi Momoyama Period. The way of tea is not just about drinking tea, but also emphasizes a spiritual exchange between the host and guests and pursues the drinking of tea in a manner that values harmony with nature. Items such as the various utensils used and of course Japanese sweets have advanced along with the way of tea, making a great contribution to the development of many facets of traditional Japanese culture.

決められた様式・作法にのっとり、客にお茶をふるまう茶道は、安土桃山時代に千利休によって大成したと言われる。ただお茶を飲むのではなく、亭主と客との精神的な交流を重視し、季節感を大切にしたもてなしがなされる。和菓子や茶道具などは茶道とともに発展し、日本の伝統文化の発展に大きく貢献した。

The spirit of tea　お茶の心

An important part of the way of tea is the feeling of consideration one should hold for other people. On the host's side, it is ideal to consider what one should do to enable the guest to pass the time pleasantly and to work out a plan to achieve this. And, on the guest's side, it is ideal to respond to the feelings of the host and display appreciation with one's words and attitude. This mutual consideration is a crucial element of the way of tea.

茶道において大切な精神は「相手のことを思う」気持ち。もてなす側は、どうしたらお客様が気持ちよく過ごせるのかを考え、趣向を凝らします。そして、もてなされた側はホストの気持ちに応え、言葉や態度で感謝の意を表します。その心のやりとりこそが最も美しく、欠けてはならないものですよ。

Mr. Randy Channell (Sōei)
ランディー・チャネル（宗榮）さん

Randy is a Canadian living in Kyoto. He came to Japan originally to study martial arts. Randy began to study the way of tea in the spirit of mastering both martial and cultural pursuits, and has since become an associate professor of the Urasenke tradition of tea. He currently holds classes in the way of tea at several places including Nashi-no-ki-jinjya and ran Hotei and gives lectures and presentations all over Japan. http://www.15-1a.com/

京都在住のカナダ人。武道を学ぶために来日。文武両道という精神から茶道を始め、裏千家準教授となる。現在は、梨木神社やらん布袋などで茶道教室を開催。http://www.15-1a.com/

There are certain meanings in the established manners of the way of tea. Try to remember some of the basics!

茶道の決められた作法にはちゃんと意味がある。基本的なものは覚えておこう!

1 Remove your watch when having tea

茶室でお茶をいただく時は、時計を外す

Remove any decorative rings, they may damage the tea utensils (wedding rings are OK…If you are carefull!)
器を傷つける可能性のある指輪も外そう(マリッジリングはOK!)

The space used to enjoy tea be it in the inside of a room or a proper teahouse is considered a world apart from everyday life. By removing your watch, you indicate your intention to value the time you are spending in the company of the other guests.

お茶を楽しむための部屋、茶室の中は日常と隔離された世界と考えられている。時計を外すことで、一緒にお茶を楽しむ人との時間を大切にしているという意思表示にもなる。

2 Drink after eating a Japanese sweet

お茶は和菓子を食べた後に飲む

Japanese sweets are made to complement the tea. Furthermore, the spirit of nature is firmly rooted in the way of tea so the sweets are often given colours and shapes that reflect the seasons and allow the participants in the gathering to enjoy not only the taste but their apperances as well.

和菓子はあくまでお茶を引き立てるものなので先に食べて。また、茶道には自然を愛し、感じようとする心が根づいているので、季節を感じられるような色や形をしている。

The sweets served change depending on the season and the theme of the gathering!
季節によって出てくるお菓子も変わるよ!

3 Avoid drinking from the front of the tea bowl

器の正面を避けて口をつける

Before drinking the tea make a slight bow of respect then turn it twice clockwise to avoid drinking from the front. When finished, wipe the bowl then turn it back twice counterclockwise!
飲む時は時計回り、戻す時は反対向きに器をずらして!

Not all bowls have an obvious front but the host will serve what he or she has selected as the front of the bowl to the guest. This shows an element of consideration from the host to the guest. As a form of consideration from the guest to the host the guest will turn the front of the bowl away before drinking from it then return the front after drinking.

お茶腕は器の正面が見えるように置かれる。これは、お茶を出す側のもてなしの心の表れ。飲む側も亭主への心遣いとして、正面をずらし口をつけて飲む。飲み終わったら器を目で楽しみ、正面に戻して元の場所に置こう。

What is Urasenke? 裏千家って?

Urasenke is one of the 3 Sen family traditions of tea (Omotesenke, Urasenke and Mushakōjisenke) to have Sen no Rikyū, who has had the deepest impact on the way of tea, as its ancestor. Urasenke currently has 98 branches and groups in 34 countries around the world, where all involved are devoted to spreading the maxim of Sen Genshitsu the 15th generation Grand Tea Master of Urasenke 'Peacefulness through a Bowl of Tea'. The style of serving tea using tables and chairs, known in Japanese as ryūrei, was developed by the 11th generation Grand Tea Master of Urasenke Gengensai.

茶道を大成した千利休を先祖に持つ3つの流派表千家・裏千家・武者小路千家)のうちのひとつ。現在最も多くの門下生を持つ流派で、伝統的な流派では珍しく新しい点前を積極的に行っている。テーブルと椅子の席で行う点前「立礼式」も裏千家から発祥。

ran Hotei らん布袋
MAP P106B2
中京区上瓦町64
☎075-801-0790
15 min walk from JR Nijō Station
http://www.ranhotei.com/

ran Hotei holds tea seminars, lectures, demonstrations, group sessions and experience tea classes. They will try to arrange the events to suit your preferred time and date. Please don't hesitate to call for more details.

お茶のセミナー講義、デモンストレーション、グループセッション、一日体験教室などが開かれる。希望の日時を相談すれば柔軟に対応してくれる。

Enjoy some tea at a temple

お寺でお茶を楽しむ

Enjoy some tea in between sightseeing after you learn the simple etiquette of the tea ceremony. You can have tea at some of the temples of Kyoto. Some temples also provide a tea-house or somewhere you can look at a garden so try asking one of the temple staff. You might even be able to understand the spirit of tea if you spend some time drinking tea slowly while you gaze out on a beautiful garden.

茶道の簡単なマナーを覚えたら、次は観光の合間にお茶を楽しもう。京都のお寺の中には、寺内でお茶がいただけるところもある。茶室や庭の見える茶席を設け

ていることもあるので、お寺の人に尋ねてみるとよいだろう。美しい庭を眺めながらゆっくりと過ごせば茶の心を理解できるかも!?

Going first thing in the morning is recommended
if you want to enjoy your time quietly!
静かに楽しみたいなら 朝一番がおすすめ！

Hōsen-in
宝泉院

The highlight of Hōsen-in is Bankan-en, a garden viewed from
the library. This style of garden is called "*gakubuchi*", meaning
picture frame, because you look at it through columns and gates
that look like a frame. You can enjoy the sight of cherry blossoms in spring and autumn colours in autumn. The Bankan-en
garden really has the beauty of a picture.

宝泉院の見所は書院からのぞむ盤桓
園（ばんかんえん）。柱と鴨居の空
間を額縁に見立てて観賞することか
ら「額縁庭園」と呼ばれる。春には
桜、秋には紅葉が楽しめ、まさに絵
画のような美しさ。

MAP　P102D1
左京区大原勝林院町187
15 min walk from Ōhara Kyoto bus stop. It is about
1 hour 5 minutes in Kyoto Bus from the Kyoto
Station square bus terminal to Ōhara.
9:00～17:00
¥ 800 (The entrance fee includes tea)

Taizō-in, a sub-temple at Myōshin-ji
妙心寺塔頭 退蔵院

This is Daihonzan Myōshin-ji, the head temple of the Rinzai Shū
Myōshin-ji sect. Taizō-in, a sub-temple at Myōshin-ji, has a tea-
house called Daikyū-an. From the tea-house, you can see Yokō-
en, a garden set out by the master gardener Kinsaku Nakane.
The azaleas, cherry blossoms, wisterias and other flowers of the
four seasons are beautiful.

臨済宗妙心寺派の大本山・妙心寺。
その塔頭である退蔵院には大休庵と
いう茶室があり、茶室からは名作庭
師の中根金作氏が手がけた庭園、余
香苑（よこうえん）が眺められる。
ツツジや桜、藤など四季折々の花が
美しい。

MAP　P111B3
右京区花園妙心寺町35
8 min walk from JR Hanazono Station
9:00～17:00
Entrance fee ¥ 500, green tea (with a sweet) ¥ 500

A pause after a stroll in the garden!
庭園を散策した後に一服！

The basics on the sweets of Kyoto

Warabi mochi (bean cakes)
わらびもち

Combine *warabi* flour, water and sugar in a pan and heat to make gruel. Cool this mixture to harden into *mochi*. It looks like jelly, but when you compare them, *mochi* is rather more elastic and glutinous. You often eat mochi covered with *kinako* or molasses.

鍋にわらび粉と水、砂糖を合わせて熱し、粘りを出す。それを冷やし固めたもの。ゼリーのような見た目だが、比較するとかなり弾力と粘りがある。きなこや黒蜜をかけて食べる。

Warabi flour わらび粉

Warabi flour is made by hardening starch taken from *warabi* rootstock and grinding it into powder. It is a luxury that can only be taken in small quantities.

わらびの根茎から採取されるデンプンを固めて粉状にしたもの。少量しか採れない高級品。

Warabi mochi toppings
わらびもちのトッピング

Kinako きなこ

Kinako is made by grinding roasted soybeans into powder. You can taste the distinctive aroma of soybeans.

焙煎した大豆を粉末にしたもの。
大豆独特の香ばしさが味わえる。

Molasses 黒蜜

This is syrup made from brown sugar lump.

黒糖から作られるシロップ。

Japanese sweets are very healthy! They are made using beans and grains rather than cream and butter. You will probably be surprised and want to know what they are made from and how.

クリームやバターを使わず、豆や穀物で作る日本のスイーツは、とてもヘルシー！でも、「何からできてるの？」「どうやって作ってるの？」と不思議に思うことも多いのでは。

Mochi rice もち米

This is a type of rice and is cultivated mainly as the raw ingredient for *mochi*. In comparison to the rice usually eaten as a staple, *mochi* rice is very elastic and viscous.

普段主食として食べられる米に比べて弾力が強く、粘度がある。

Mochi rice cakes もち

Mochi are made by pounding steamed *mochi* rice until it sticks together and then forming it into round or flat shapes. *Mochi* can be eaten on an everyday basis and they are also used as offerings for celebrations and happy events as well as Shintō and Buddhist rituals.

蒸したもち米をつき、丸や平らにする。祝事、慶事、神事、仏事などに供物としても使われる。

Zenzai
ぜんざい

Zenzai is a soup made by floating *mochi* or rice flour dumplings (dumplings made from *mochi* rice ground into flour) in azuki beans boiled sweetly using more water than for making an bean jam. *Zenzai* is very sweet so it is often accompanied by something like salty *konbu* or *konbu* boiled in soy sauce as a palate freshener.

あんより水分を多くして甘く煮た小豆に、もちや白玉を浮かべたもの。口直しに塩昆布や佃煮などを添えることが多い。

Azuki 小豆

Azuki beans are an essential for Japanese sweets and are the raw material for *anko* bean jam.

和菓子に欠かせないあんこの原料となる豆。

Hōsen
宝泉
MAP　P109E1
15 min walk from Kitaōji Station on the
Karasuma subway line
10:00〜17:00
Closed：Wed

An あん

An bean jam is made by boiling *azuki* beans with water and sugar. An bean jam is divided largely into two types. One is known as *tsubu-an* and contains lumps of *azuki* bean, and the other is known as *koshi-an* and is smooth. The skins are scraped off the *azuki* beans to make the smooth *koshi-an*.

小豆を水、砂糖で煮たもの。小豆の粒が残った粒あんと、こして粒の残さないこしあんに分けられる。

A short break on a kawayuka riverside platform

川床でひと休み

A *kawayuka* is a temporary platform established above a river for the enjoyment of food and drink and to cool down when summer comes. During the period from May to the end of September every year, the eating and drinking establishments lined up along the Kamo River set up temporary terrace areas known as *nōryōyuka*, which are used by many people.

毎年5～9月の間、鴨川沿いに並ぶ飲食店が仮設のテラス席「納涼床」を出し、多くの人に利用されている。

Couples spread out at equal intervals along the Kamo River
鴨川・等間隔カップル♥

The Kamo River runs north-south through Kyoto City. As the evening closes in, couples sit at equally-spaced intervals along the side of the river between the Shijō and Sanjō roads to talk about love. The more couples there are, the narrower the spaces between them become. Whether you watch cheerfully from Shijō Bridge or look on enviously is down to your heart and situation.

夕暮れ時が近づくと、四条から三条間の川沿いになぜか等間隔にカップルが座り愛を語り合う。並ぶカップルの数が多くなるほど間隔も狭まる。ほほえましく見守るのか嫉妬と羨望のまなざしで見るのかは、あなたの心と状況次第で。

Where are the restaurants visitors can enjoy a kawayuka riverside platform?

Starbucks Coffee Kyoto Sanjō-ōhashi branch
スターバックス コーヒー 京都三条大橋店

Even the familiar Starbucks sets up a *kawayuka* to create a Kyoto style.

お馴染みスターバックスも、川床を出して京都風に。

MAP   P107E2
中京区三条通河原町東入中島町
113 近江屋ビル1F
1 min walk from Keihan Sanjō Station
8:00〜24:00,〜 25:00 Fri and Sat

Ikumatsu
幾松

Have an orthodox Japanese meal on a *kawayuka* riverside platform at an historic gourmet inn.

歴史ある料理旅館の正統派和食を川床で。

MAP   P107E2
中京区木屋町御池上ル
10 min walk from Keihan Sanjō Station
11:30〜15:30, 17:30〜19:30
¥5500〜（lunch）,¥14000〜（dinner）

BAR ATLANTIS

How about a glass or two while listening to the babble of the Kamo River?

鴨川のせせらぎを聞きながらグラスを傾けてみては？

MAP   P107E3
中京区四条先斗町上ル松本町161
3 min walk from Keihan Shijō Station
18:00〜26:00,〜25:00 on Sun (Kawa yuka riverside platform until 23:00)
Budget ¥2500〜,
Table charge ¥1000

なんて便利！！指さしメニュー

Keiran udon noodles
けいらんうどん

Egg is added to a thick sauce (broth thickened with potato starch), heated and served on top of *udon* noodles.

片栗粉でとろみをつけたあんかけに卵を入れ火を通したものが、うどんの上にのる。

Soba noodles with nishin
にしんそば

A dried herring (dried after the removal of its innards) is boiled in a saltened, sweetened broth and served on top of buckwheat *soba* noodles.

身欠きにしん（内臓を取り除き、乾燥させたもの）を、甘辛く煮たものがそばの上にのる。

Chicken Namba soba noodles
鳥なんばそば

Buckwheat *soba* noodles with chicken and cibols. *Namba* is a general nickname attached to things handed down from regions in the south of Japan. This word is often used to mean that the dish contains chili and cibols.

鶏肉とねぎの入ったそば。ネーミングの由来は、唐辛子やねぎを「なんば」と呼んでいたことにある。

Shippoku udon noodles
しっぽくうどん

Udon noodles with extras such as slices of fish sausage, Japanese omelette, marinated *shiitake* mushrooms, bamboo shoot, etc.

かまぼこ、薄焼き卵、味つけしたしいたけ、タケノコなどの具が載ったうどん。

Oyako-don
親子丼

A topping made of pieces of chicken and held together with egg is served on top of rice. *Oyako-don*, means "the parent-child bowl"because it is made of chicken (the parent) and egg (the child).

鶏肉を卵でとじた丼。鶏（親）と卵（子）だから親子丼と呼ばれる。

Gontaro Okazaki branch
権太呂 岡崎店

Apart from Okazaki, Gontaro also has branches in Shijō Fuyachō and close to Kinkaku-ji.

岡崎以外に四条麩屋町、金閣寺付近にも店舗がある。

MAP P107F1
左京区岡崎南御所町19
5 min walk from the Dōbutsuen-mae city bus stop
11：00～22：00
Budged:￥700～

Udon noodles

Udon noodles are made by kneading flour and water. They are often served in a hot soup made by flavouring a broth made from kelp or dried bonito with ingredients such as soy sauce and *mirin*. In summer, *udon* noodles are often eaten dipped in a cold, heavily flavoured soup or topped with a sauce of some kind.

Buckwheat soba noodles

Soba noodles are made using flour ground from buckwheat grains. *Soba* noodles are eaten in the same way as *udon* noodles. *Soba* noodles contain much more dietary fiber and vitamins than *udon* and have a high nutritional value.

There are no English menus at a lot of restaurants and drinking holes! Even if there is a menu, you can't understand the explanation ... If you find yourself in such a place, point at what you want on this page and show the waiter or waitress to make your order smoothly. Noodles, which can be eaten casually, are just right for lunch.

Kotteri(=rich) rāmen
こってりラーメン

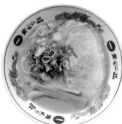

Kotteri rāmen is the standard dish at this restaurant. Dozens of types of vegetables are added to chicken carcass stock to make a soup like a potage that is boiled over a long period of time.

この店の定番メニュー。鶏ガラと数十種類の野菜を長時間煮込んだスープは、ポタージュのよう。

Assari(=light) rāmen
あっさりラーメン

This is the general type of *rāmen* available in Japan. Its chicken carcass stock flavoured with a soy sauce base, gives a delicious, fresh flavour.

醤油ベースの鶏ガラスープであっさりとした味わい。

Rice
白ごはん

Rice is often eaten alongside *rāmen*. Order rice when you feel *rāmen* will not be enough, but you don't think you can finish off a bowl of fried rice.

ラーメンのお供に。

Gyōza
餃子

Gyōza pork dumplings are popular as a side dish. In Japan, *gyōza* dumplings are usually fried and often contain garlic.

サイドメニューとして人気。日本では焼き餃子が一般的で、具にニンニクが入っているものが多い。

Fried rice
炒飯

This is a standard dish on menus, comprised of ingredients such as Chinese-style barbecued pork, cibols and egg fried with white rice.

チャーシューやねぎ、卵などをごはんと一緒に炒めたごはん。

Tenka Ippin head branch (Kitashirakawa)
天下一品 総本店（北白川）

Tenka Ippin has developed as a chain and there are restaurants in many locations. It is easy to find with its garish shop signs.

チェーン展開しており、各所に店舗がある。
派手な看板を目印に。

MAP P102D3
左京区一乗寺築田町94メゾン白川1F
5 min walk from the Kyoto Zōkei Daigaku-mae city bus stop 11：00～27：00 Closed: Thu Budged：¥630～

Seasoning agents

Use Seasoning agents when you want to adjust a dish to suit your tastes. They may change the flavour significantly so add these seasoning agents a little bit at a time while keeping track of the flavour. From the left, there are *rāyu* (mix a little *rāyu* into *gyōza* sauce), *gyōza* sauce, salt (for boiled eggs and vegetables eaten as an accompaniment), pepper (to add spice to your *rāmen*), *rāmen* sauce (when the flavour of your *rāmen* is weak) and chili powder (when you want to add some heat and depth to your *rāmen*).

Rāmen

Rāmen is a noodle dish that originated in China. Egg noodles are placed in a Chinese soup made from chicken carcass and pork bones, with ingredients such as Chinese-style barbecued pork, cibols, and sungan placed on top. Despite originating in China, *rāmen* has achieved development into something uniquely Japanese.

63

Recommended shopping unique to Kyoto!

京都ならではのお勧めグッズはコレ！

Shopping is one of the pleasures of being on holiday. Products that you can use on an everyday basis while also feeling the atmosphere of Kyoto make perfect gifts for yourself and for others. Take the feeling of Kyoto home with you.

旅先での楽しみのひとつである買い物。京都らしさを感じさせつつも、普段も使えるグッズは自分用にもみやげ用にもぴったり。

Kyōyūzen aloha shirts
京友禅アロハシャツ

These aloha shirts are slightly different from the showy aloha shirts that conjure up images of sun and sand. These are aloha shirts dyed in the Kyōyūzen style by the Kameda Tomisen factory, which has been involved in *kimono* dyeing for many years.

派手で陽気なイメージのアロハとはひと味違うこのアロハシャツ。長年着物の染色に携わってきた亀田富染工場が手がけたもので、友禅染めの技術を生かしたアロハなのだ。

Pagong Gion branch パゴン 祇園店
MAP　P107E3
東山区八坂新地清本町373
3 min walk from Keihan Shijō Station
11：30〜20：00
Closed: Wed
Kyōyuzen aloha shirts ￥18900〜

Kyōyūzen dyeing denim
友禅染めデニム

Denim dyed with Japanese images such as *rangiku* (chrysanthemum flowers blooming wildly) and phoenixes. Denim made using the dyeing techniques and processing technology of ancient Japan such as Kyōyūzen dyeing is also great value and brilliant for making clothes.

乱菊(乱れ咲く菊の花の模様)や鳳凰などの和柄が描かれたデニム。友禅染めなど日本古来の染色技術や加工技術が駆使されたデニムは、ボトムラインや縫製も秀逸。

mizra ミズラ
MAP　P107D2
中京区富小路通三条下ル朝倉町536
7 min walk from Karasuma Oike Station on the Karasuma subway line
13：00〜20：00(11：00〜 Sat, Sun and public holidays)
Closed: Tues　Kyōyūzen dyeing denim ￥35700〜

Incense インセンス

More than 150 types of colorful incense sticks are on display in this shop. You may want to buy a stylish incense holder as well.

お店には150種以上ものカラフルなスティックインセンスが並ぶ。スタイリッシュなインセンスホルダーと一緒に買いたい。

lisn
MAP　P106C3
下京区烏丸通四条下ルCOCON烏丸1F
1 min walk from Karasuma Shijō Station on the Karasuma subway line
11：00〜20：00
Closed：Shop holidays not fixed
¥315(10 incenses)〜

Chiyogami paper 千代紙

Japanese paper from all over the country and tens of thousands of types of Chiyogami are available at this shop. Chiyogami are dyed with *kimono* patterns including Kaga-yūzen and Kyōchiyo styles using wooden printing blocks and stamps, etc, and allow you to readily enjoy the atmosphere of Japanese designs.

この店には、日本各地の和紙や何万種類もの千代紙が揃う。千代紙は加賀友禅や京千代などの着物の柄が木版や型などで染められ、和柄の雰囲気を手軽に楽しむことができる。

Morita Wagami　森田和紙
MAP　P106C3
下京区東洞院通仏光寺上ル扇酒屋町298
3 min walk from Shijō Station on the Karasuma subway line
9：30〜17：30(〜16：30 Sat)
Closed: Sun & holiday
Chiyogami ¥200〜

Nishijin purse 西陣織の小銭入れ

Shōsuikaku is an art gallery started by *obi* makers boasting world-class weaving technology. The gallery sells not only *obi* and *kimono*, but also a range of smaller products that incorporate intricate designs using gold and platinum thread that glitter beautifully.

松翠閣は世界に誇る織りの技術を持つ帯屋が始めた美術館。帯や掛け軸はもちろん、小さなグッズにも細やかな柄が金糸やプラチナ縛で織り込まれ、きらきらと美しい。

Shōsuikaku　松翠閣
MAP　P108B2
上京区寺之内通智恵光院東入ル北側
10 min walk from the Horikawa Teranouchi city bus stop
9：30〜17：00　Nisijin purse ¥1600

Perfumed bag straps 匂袋ストラップ

Small perfumed bags transmit perfume fragrances to clothes, and aromas can be enjoyed at any time. These perfumed bags are made for use as straps on mobile phones.

香料を小さな袋に包んだ匂袋は、衣服に香りを移したり香りを楽しんだりする。これは、匂袋を携帯電話のストラップ用にしたもの。

Kyūkyodō 鳩居堂
MAP　P107D2
中京区寺町姉小路上ル下本能寺前町520
4 min walk from Kyoto Shiyakusho-mae Station on the Karasuma subway line
10：00〜18：00
Closed: Sun　Perfumed bag straps ¥788〜

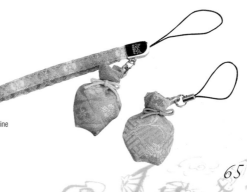

How to use a tenugui towel

A *tenugui* is a towel made of a material such as cotton. *Tenugui* towels are thin yet strong, are used in various ways such as to wipe the face or wrap objects, and can be convenient to carry one around with you. They come in all sorts of colours and designs, and some have also appeared with old patterns given a contemporary look.

Wrapping objects
包む

Tenugui towels are convenient for wrapping small objects. They can be used as a fashionable way of wrapping plastic beverage bottles, and will also absorb condensation in summer and provide an insulating effect in winter.

ちょっとした物を包むのに便利。ボトルケースとしてペットボトルを包めばおしゃれな上、夏場は水滴を吸ってくれるし、冬なら保温効果もある。

As neckwear
ネックウェアとして

You can also wrap *Tenugui* towels around your neck like a scarf and use them as neckwear. Linen *Tenugui* towels, which possess a nice touch, also absorb perspiration and provide protection from the cold.

マフラーやスカーフのように首に巻けば、ネックウェアに。肌触りのいいガーゼ地のものなら、汗を吸収してくれるし、防寒にもなる。

As a tissue case
ティッシュケースとして

A drab box of tissues wrapped with a fancy *tenugui* towel will become a part of your home's interior decorations. First, place a box of tissues in the center of a spread out *tenugui* towel, and fold the four corners in to match the height of the box. Next, all you have to do is tie up the ends.

味気のないティッシュ箱を手ぬぐいで包んで部屋のインテリアの一部に。まずは、広げた手ぬぐいの中央部にティッシュを置き、箱の高さに合わせて四方の生地を折りこむ。あとは端を結ぶだけ。

How to use a furoshiki

ふろしきの使い方

The *furoshiki*, which has been used as an everyday item in Japan throughout the ages, is a cloth used for wrapping and carrying objects. Recently, they have also been attracting attention as ecobags that can be used over and over again. Try being creative with the way you wrap objects and use a *furoshiki* with style.

1 Tie a single knot at one end of the *furoshiki*. Tie the other three ends in the same way.

ふろしきの端をひとつ結びする。他の3つの端も同様にひとつ結びにする。

2 Tie a square knot in adjacent corners to make a carrying handle.

持ち手を作るために、隣り合う隅の先端を真結びする。

3 When you tie the opposite side, your *furoshiki* bag will be complete.

反対側も結べば、ふろしきバッグのできあがり。

RAAK ラーク
MAP PP106C2
中京区室町通姉小路下ル役行者町358
3 min walk from Karasuma Oike Station
on the Karasuma subway line
11:00〜19:00
tenugui ￥1575
froshiki ￥2625

Take a walk through the Nishiki Market

Hatanoken Rōho 畑野軒老舗

Our recommendation here is raw gluten buns. Made using gluten obtained from flour, these buns are really soft. The filling of these chewy buns is koshian red bean paste.

10:00～18:00
Closed: Wed

お勧めは生麩のまんじゅう。小麦粉のグルテンから作られ、モチモチとしている。噛みごたえのあるまんじゅうの中にはこし餡が入る。

Ikemasa-tei いけまさ亭

Our recommendation at Ikemasa-tei is seasonal set lunches. Ikemasa-tei is a restaurant established inside a greengrocery. You can try *obanzai* cuisine made using seasonal Kyoto vegetables. At lunchtime, customers can order set lunches, which change monthly, and at nighttime choose from an a-la-carte menu.

八百屋の中にある食事処で、旬の京野菜を使ったおばんざいが食べられる。昼は月替わりの定食、夜は単品で頼める。

11:30～14:00,17:30～21:30
Closed: Tues, the evening of Sun, Mon

（餅・和菓子）畑野軒老舗

（豆腐）こんなもんじゃ

Takakura-dōri

Sakaimachi-dōri

Yanagi-no-banba-dōri

（おばんざい）いけまさ亭

Tomi-no-kōji-dōri

池鶴果実（果物）

Konna Mon Ja こんなもんじゃ

Konna Mon Ja is run under the direct management of Fujino, the *Kyōtōfu* specialist, and sells sweets made using soymilk. Try taking a walk along the market eating bite-sized soymilkdoughnuts fried in quick succession, or a soymilk ice cream.

豆腐屋の京とうふ藤野の直営店で豆乳を使ったスイーツが揃う。次々と揚げられるひと口サイズの豆乳ドーナツや豆乳ソフトクリームを食べ歩きしよう。
10:00～19:00

Iketsuru Fruit Store 池鶴果実

Customers can order fruit juice made from the more than 30 types of fruit available in this store. It is also possible to combine 2 or more types of fruits to make mixed fruit juices. Try dropping in when you take a walk through the Nishiki Market.

店頭に並ぶ30種以上の果物をジュースにして飲むことができる。2種類以上の果物を合わせてミックスジュースにもできる。　9:00～18:30　Closed: Wed

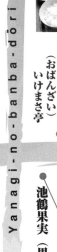

The Nishiki Market extends for 390m through the center of Kyoto. Shops selling fresh foodstuffs such as fish have lined this marketplace for many years, and the area is also known as Kyoto's kitchen. If you wish to experience Kyoto more deeply, try visiting these shops that are firmly rooted in the local community. Here we introduce from among the many shops in the Nishiki Market, some of those we recommend for Kyoto-style items as well as eating and walking trips.

京都の中心地にて全長390mも続く錦市場。古くより魚など生鮮食品の店が並び、京都の台所と呼ばれる。数あるお店から京都らしいもの、食べ歩きにお勧めなお店をご紹介。

Yamadashiya やまだしや

Our recommendation at Yamadashiya is coarse tea. Japanese people regularly drink green tea. Yamadashiya sells different varieties such as *hōjicha* roasted green tea alongside standard *ryokucha* green tea. The fragrance that drifts from the roasting machines that work all day long smells very nice.

日本人が普段よく口にする飲み物、ほうじ茶や緑茶などの茶葉を販売。1日中動き続ける、茶を焙じる機械からいい香りが漂う。

10:00～18:00
Closed: Wed

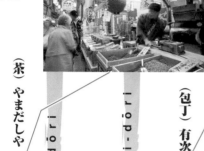

（茶）やまだしや

Nishikikōji -dōri

Fuyachō-dōri

大藤（漬物）

Gokōmachi-dōri

（包丁）有次

Teramachi-dōri

（焼きあなご）まるやた

Shinkyōgoku-dōri

Aritsugu 有次

Aritsugu, which boasts a history of more than 440 years, sells kitchen utensils such as knives as well as pots and dies made by craftsmen. If you buy a knife you can also have your name engraved on the blade.

創業440年以上もの歴史を誇る有次では、包丁を始め職人手作りの鍋や抜き型などの料理道具が揃う。また、買った包丁に名入れのサービスも。

9:00～17:30
※Check that you can take the knives back to your own country.

Maruyata grilled eel restaurant
焼きあなご まるやた

Our recommendation at Maruyata is eel on rice. Visit this restaurant if you want to savor the taste of Japanese seafood. You can try a rice-bowl topped with eel loaded with fat and grilled over charcoal to give a crunchy skin and soft inner meat, as well as *sushi*.

名物は焼きあなご丼。脂ののったあなごを皮はパリッと、中はふんわりと炭火で焼いた丼や寿司が食べられる。

11:30～16:00,
18:00～19:30
Closed: Wed

Daitō 大藤

Our recommendation at Daitō is *senmaizuke* pickled radishes. This is a traditional Kyoto pickle and the ones you can purchase at Daitō are the original. *Senmaizuke* is made by thinly slicing Shōgō-in radishes and lightly pickling them in kelp, vinegar and sugar. However, if you do buy some please be aware that they have a short shelf life.

京都伝統の漬物、千枚漬の元祖。千枚漬とは聖護院かぶらを薄く切り、昆布や酢、砂糖で浅漬けにしたもの。ただし、日持ちがしないので注意。

MAP P107D3 8:00～18:00

To the markets

Kitano Tenman-gū 北野天満宮
MAP　P111C2　上京区馬喰町
1 min walk from the Kitano Tenman-gū-mae city bus stop

Tenjin Market
天神市

This is the antique market held at Kitano Tenman-gū. After you pass through the shrine gate there are stalls for food and games on the shrine pathways that give the air of a street market. Around the pathways, there are stores selling secondhand clothes and antique *kimonos* as well as other antiques. The Tenjin Market is held on the 25th of each month from 6am to 17pm.

北野天満宮の骨董市。鳥居をくぐった先の参道では縁日らしい食べ物やゲームなどの屋台が出店。参道のまわりでは古着やアンティーク着物、骨董の店が並ぶ。毎月25日の6〜17時ごろまで開催。

Kōbō Market
弘法市

This is the street market held at Tō-ji. More than 1000 stalls sell a wide variety of goods including plants, food, antiques, secondhand clothes, and miscellaneous goods, etc. The Kōbō Market is held on the 21st of each month from 8am to about 16pm.

東寺の縁日。植木や食品、骨董、古着、雑貨などバラエティのある出店で、その数は1000以上。毎月21日の8〜16時ごろまで開催。

Tō-ji 東寺
MAP　P104A3　南区九条町1
15 min walk from JR Kyoto Station

Kyoto, a town that protects the good things of old, is replete with antique markets. Unlike flea markets, traders also give proper guarantees for products from their stores.

古きよきものを守る街・京都はアンティークマーケットも充実。フリーマーケットとは違い、業者さんが出店するから品物もきちんと保証されている。

Daruma Street
ダルマストリート

Daruma Street is the name for the area between the street that extends westwards from the new gate of Chion-in and the street one block north in front of the old gate. There are now many shops that sell antiques and art, and the area is known as an artistic neighbourhood. The area is called Daruma Street because of the Daruma signs that hang there.

知恩院から西へ伸びる新門前通とその1本北の通りの古門前通。今や骨董や美術品を扱う店が多く美術の街とされる。通りにかかるダルマの看板からダルマストリートと呼ばれる。

MAP　P107E2

Gojō-zaka Pottery Fair
五条坂陶器祭

This is a large-scale pottery market with as many as 500 pottery stalls lining the northern and southern sides of a stretch of Gojō-zaka from Gojō-ōhashi to Higashiōji, and is a feature of Kyoto's summers. On the northern side are older, established stalls, and on the southern side, the stalls of younger potters. The fair is typically held from about the 7th to the 10th of August.

五条大橋から東大路通の南北の五条坂一帯に500もの陶器店が出店する大陶器市で、京都の夏の風物詩のひとつ。北側は老舗のお店、南側は若手作家の店が並ぶ。例年8月7日〜10日開催。

MAP　P107E4

Visit a Kyotoesque house

京都らしい町家へ行こう

Shōki しょうき

A *shōki*, which has a scary face and sits on top of a building's roof, is a stone figure of a god. It is supposed to be effective as a charm that protects houses against evil.

怖い顔で屋根の上に立つしょうきは神様の石像。家を守る魔よけの効能があるとされる。

Inuyarai 犬矢来

An *inuyarai* is a protective barrier found on the lower parts of *machiya*. An *inuyarai* is generally made from bamboo and protects the walls of houses from splashing rain and damage.

塀の下方にある円弧状の垣根。竹製が一般的で、家の壁を雨の跳ね返りや外部からの損傷から防ぐ。

Machiya Italian
町家イタリアン

There are restaurants where you can dine on Italian food while experiencing the attraction of a *machiya* ... the external appearance with a trellis and *Mushiko*, dirt walls and pillars that evoke history in their naked beams, and beautiful, well-kept gardens. Depending on the establishment tables and chairs are used, so you do not have to worry about the discomfort of sitting in the *seiza* position (on your knees).

格子や虫籠などの外観、土壁やむきだしの梁に歴史を感じさせる柱、丁寧に手入れされた美しい中庭…町家風情を感じながら、イタリア料理を食べることができるレストラン。この店に限らず、店によってはテーブル席もあるから正座の辛さに悩まされることもない。

A *machiya* is a building constructed in a style that has been handed down from olden times in Kyoto. Many *machiya* combine the owner's residence and business. In recent years, the beauty of these classic buildings has been reappraised, and they have attracted attention following transformations into restaurants, cafes, and galleries, etc.

町家とは京都に古くから伝わるスタイルの建築物で、多くが住居と店とを兼ねていた。近年、その建築美が見直され、飲食店やカフェ、ギャラリーなどへと形を変えて注目を集めている。

Mushiko 虫籠

Mushiko is a grilled window built into 2nd floor walls for the purposes of ventilation and lighting. The origin of the name is supposedly found in the similarity of the shapes of these windows with insect cages.

通風や採光を目的に2階にある塗り壁に施される。ネーミングの由来は、その形が虫かごに似ているからとされる。

Trellis 格子

A trellis, which also shows a *machiya* off with style, is a structure that makes it difficult to see inside from outside, and easy to see outside from inside.

町家をスタイリッシュに見せる格子は、外からは中が見えにくく、中からは外が見やすい造り。

The small courtyard garden, unique to the *machiya* style, is beautiful.

町家ならではの坪庭が美しい。

Osteria Ao オステリア蒼

MAP P106C2
中京区室町通三条上ル
5 min walk from Karasuma Oike Station on the Karasuma subway line
11:30〜14:00(LO)
18:00〜21:00(LO)
Closed: Wed, 1st Tues of each month

Budget for around ¥4000 for lunch and around ¥8000 for dinner

予算は約¥4000(ランチ)、約¥8000(ディナー)。

Read some manga!

Chōjū-jinbutsu-giga goods 鳥獣人物戯画グッズ

Various manga goods are on sale in the museum shop. Among them are many with images from *Chōjū-jinbutsu-giga*, Japan's oldest manga. *Chōjū-jinbutsu-giga* is a picture scroll that personalizes animals such as rabbits and frogs, and satirizes the world. A replica of this picture scroll is on display in the museum. You must check it out!

ミュージアム内のショップには、さまざまなマンガのグッズが売られている。中には、日本最古のマンガともされる鳥獣人物戯画が描かれたグッズも数多く揃う。鳥獣人物戯画とは、ウサギやカエルなどの動物を擬人化し、世の中を風刺した絵物。館内にはこの絵物のレプリカも展示されているので、要チェック！

Miniature rolled book ¥4095
mobile phone strap ¥924
small *furoshiki* cloth wrapper ¥630

縮小巻子¥4095、携帯ストラップ¥924、小
風呂敷¥630

Manga comics are part of Japan's proud culture. At the same time, it is no exaggeration to say that Japanese manga are the best in the world. The world of manga is deep, including the creation of the new word 'otaku' (someone who loves manga), the explosive commercial popularity of character goods, and people dressing up as their favourite characters.

日本が世界に誇るべき文化のひとつ・マンガ。日本のマンガのレベルは世界一と言っても過言ではない。オタク（＝マンガ愛好家）という言葉が生まれたり、キャラクターグッズが爆発的に売れたり、お気に入りのキャラクターの扮装をして楽しんだり、とマンガの世界は奥が深い。

Kyoto International Manga Museum
京都国際マンガミュージアム

This museum was opened in the heart of Kyoto in November 2006. Inside you will find everything from valuable old manga to currently popular manga as well as manga from around the world. The museum has about 200000 manga in total.

2006年11月、京都の中心地に開館された博物館。館内には、資料として価値のある昔のマンガから現在の人気マンガ、世界各国のマンガと約20万点ものマンガが揃う。

MAP P106C2
中京区烏丸通御池上ル
1 min walk from Karasuma Oike Station on
the Karasuma subway line
10：00～20：00
Closed:Wed
Entrance fee ￥500

Fun cosplay goods

ICHI-
BAN!

Warning !

This is a warning about any sword that you buy as a memento of Kyoto. Even if it is a fake, be careful when you go home. You cannot take any sword on board a plane and you will need to tell the airline or the check-in counter that you have a fake sword with you. Also check that you can take a sword back to your own country.

模造刀でも持ち帰りには注意。飛行機内には持ち込めないし、航空会社カウンターなどで模造刀の所持を伝えなければならない。また、自国に持って帰ることができるかも確認しよう。

T-shirts with Number One written on the front in Japanese, *happi* coats, *hachimaki* headbands, old style *chonmage* and *geisha* wigs, red lanterns and swords - Japanese people use these goods when they want to liven up a party. You can get them at souvenir stores in Kyoto.

「一番」と漢字で書かれたTシャツにハッピ、ハチマキ、ちょんまげカツラに芸者カツラ、ちょうちんに刀。日本人はパーティーなどを盛り上げたい時に使う。お土産屋さんで手に入る。

Warning !

Kimonos are beautiful if they are worn properly, but you might be embarrassed if you put one on wrongly. Please be careful because wearing a *kimono* with the right side placed on top of the left side, a style called *hidarimae*, is how the dead are dressed for burial.

着物は正しく着れば美しいけれど、間違って着てしまえば恥をかくこともある。左前と言われる右襟を左襟の上に重ねる着方は、死人の装束とされるので注意。

Stay at a ryokan

Welcome! Come in.
ようこそおいでやす

Hiiragiya Bekkan 柊家別館
MAP ▶P.107D1
中京区御幸町二条下ル山本町431
☎075-231-0151
5 min walk from Kyoto Shiyakusho-mae Station on the Tôzai subway line
Per person per night inc. 2 meals: ¥ 15000〜
http://www.hiiragiya.com/

What is a ryokan?

A *ryokan* is a uniquely Japanese accommodation facility founded on the spirit of entertainment for and looking after its guests. The staff member in charge of your room, known as a *nakai*, will look after your various needs while you are staying at a *ryokan*, including bringing your meals and laying out your *futon*. Also, because the general rule is to have dinner and breakfast in your room, a *ryokan* does not have drinking and eating facilities such as restaurants. Nobody other than guests staying at the *ryokan* is allowed to enter so you can even wear *yukata* in the lobby and corridors!

旅館とは？

お客をもてなす・お世話するという精神の根づいた日本独特の宿泊施設。「仲居」と呼ばれる専属の客室係が食事や布団の準備など、さまざまなお世話をしてくれる。また、夕食・朝食の2食つきが基本なので館内に飲食施設はないことが多い。宿泊客以外入れないのでロビーや廊下でも浴衣姿でOK！

A ryokan is like this

1 When you arrive in your room, the *nakai* will make you some tea. Sweets are often served as well.

部屋につくと仲居さんがお茶を入れてくれる。お菓子もついてくることが多い。

FREE!

2 Have dinner in your room. Your room is your private space so you can put on the *yukata* laid out in the room and relax.

食事は客室で。プライベート空間だから、部屋に備えてある浴衣などのリラックスしたスタイルでOK。

Drinks during meals are charged separately!
食事中の飲み物は別料金！

3 Often, the bath is not in your room. Use the common bath or the bath for each room. Remember to take a towel and change of clothes!

お風呂は部屋にないことが多い。大浴場や客室単位で入る風呂を使おう。部屋に置いてあるタオルや着替えなどを忘れずに！

4 The *nakai* will lay out your *futon* while you are in the bath.The *nakai* will bring a pot of cold water when coming to lay out your *futon*.

お風呂に行っている間に仲居さんが布団を敷いてくれる。布団を敷きに来る時に一緒にポットを持ってきてくれる。中には冷水が入っている。

Things to remember when staying at a ryokan
旅館に泊まる時の注意

Take your shoes off at the entrance and change into slippers.

土足は厳禁！靴は玄関で脱いで、スリッパに履きかえる。

The drinks in the refrigerator are charged for.

冷蔵庫の中の飲み物は有料。

If you do not know something, ask the *nakai*!
分からなかったら仲居さんに聞こう！

You must not take items such as the *yukata* and towels home. However, you may often be able to take home a hand towel with the logo of the *ryokan* on it.

浴衣やバスタオルなどは持ち帰ってはダメ。ただし、宿のロゴ入りのハンドタオルはOKの場合が多い。

Stay in a temple lodge

宿坊に泊まろう

If you go to all the trouble of visiting Kyoto, why not stay at a temple? Apart from cheap rates, at some temples, you can also relax and enjoy national treasures, buildings classed as important cultural properties and gardens. Such stays are perfect for people interested in culture.

Temple lodges are accommodation facilities built alongside temples. They were originally used by monks coming to pray. The lodges differ depending on the temple, but at some, you can participate in religious devotions called *o-tsutome*. These devotions include facing Buddha and reading sutras early in the morning, and practicing Zazen. You can also try vegetarian cuisine at temple lodgings that serve meals.

せっかく京都に来たのなら、お寺に泊まってみては？低料金で泊まれるうえ、国宝や重要文化財の建物、庭園などがゆっくりと楽しめる寺院もあるから文化に触れたい人にはぴったり。

宿坊はお寺に併設された宿泊施設で、元々参詣にきた僧坊が利用していた。寺院によって内容は違うが、早朝、仏に向かってお経を読む、坐禅をするなどのお勤めと呼ばれる宗教儀式に参加できるところもある。食事付きの宿坊では精進料理を楽しめることも。

Cleanses the spirit, doesn't it?
心が洗われるね！

You can find many interesting things at temple lodges, from cultural property such as stone gardens and *fusuma-e* sliding door paintings, to unusual flowers such as the camellias at Myōren-ji and cherry trees that blossom when it is cold.

石庭、襖絵のような文化財から、妙蓮寺椿や寒い時期に咲く桜などの珍しい花まで見所が多い

Myōren-ji 妙蓮寺
MAP　P108B2
上京区寺之内通大宮東入ル妙蓮寺前町875
☎075-451-3527
3 min walk from the Horikawa Teranouchi bus stop
IN 18:00～20:00　OUT 9:00
¥3800（Staying overnight without meals）
http://www.eonet.ne.jp/~myorenji/

① There are no reception desks at temples. At Myōren-ji, speak to somebody in the office to check-in. Temples have curfews so check-in by evening.

フロントはない。妙蓮寺では事務室の方に声をかけ、チェックインをする。門限があるので、夕方までには宿泊の手続きをすませたい。

② Temples are holy places. Wearing shoes inside is forbidden so take your shoes off at the designated place and put them in the shoe box.

寺院は神聖な場所。土足厳禁なので所定の場所できちんと靴を脱ぎ、靴箱にしまって。

③ Rooms are simple. They have no lock or safe so look after valuables carefully.

部屋はシンプルな造り。鍵はかからず金庫もないので、貴重品の管理には気をつけよう。

④ There is often a *sentō* public bath close to a temple. The charge for using a local *sentō* is included in the bill at Myōren-ji. Make sure to get the ticket shown in the photo and go for a bath. See P.44-45 for *sentō* etiquette.

お寺の周りには銭湯があることが多い。妙蓮寺では宿泊費に銭湯の利用料金も含まれているので、ぜひ写真のチケットを手に銭湯へ行こう。銭湯でのマナーはP44・45へ。

⑤ Although the early morning *o-tsutome* rituals differ depending on the sect, you can probably still participate. Because the activities differ, you should check what they are in advance. Temples vary - at some, lodgers cannot participate and at others you must.

早朝のお勤めは宗教や宗派が違っても参加可能。宗派により内容が違うので、前もって確認しておこう。宿泊客はお勤めに参加できない、必ず参加しなければならないところなどさまざま。

⑥ Pay the bill when you check out. However, if you are leaving early in the morning when the office is closed, pay the day before.

宿泊費の精算はチェックアウト時に。ただ、事務室が開いていない早朝に出発をするならば前日に支払いを済ませておこう。

Points to note when staying at a temple lodge
宿坊に泊まる時の注意

Make sure to book 予約は必ずしよう
Most of the time, you cannot suddenly decide to stay at a temple lodge. You need to book ahead. Also, when you stay at a temple lodge, it is better to go with somebody who can speak Japanese.

急に「泊まりたい」と言っても無理な場合がほとんど。また、宿泊する時は、日本語を話せる人と一緒のほうがベター。

Observe the set curfew 設定された門限を守る
There is no receptionist constantly available, like at a hotel. You will offend people if you are late so observe the set time properly.

ホテルのように常にフロント係がいるわけではない。時間に遅れたら迷惑がかかるので、ちゃんと決められた時間を守って。

Bring what you need
アメニティグッズは自分で用意する
Most places do not have dressing gowns or toiletries. Bring what you need.

寝間着や洗面用具などの用意がない施設がほとんど。必要なものは自分で用意を。

Be quiet はしゃぎすぎない
Most old temples are not insulated against sound. Be quiet at night so that you do not bother other guests. Go to bed and wake up early and take part in the morning *o-tsutome* rituals.

古いお寺の場合、防音設備が整えられていないことが多い。他の客の迷惑にならないよう、夜は静かに。早寝早起きをして、朝のお勤めに参加しよう。

Stay at a guesthouse

ゲストハウスに泊まる

If you intend to stay in Kyoto for a week or longer, you might like to consider using a guesthouse. Rates are reasonable and another attraction is that you can feel what it is like to live in Kyoto.

1週間以上の長期滞在をするなら、ゲストハウスを利用するという手もある。価格がリーズナブルというのはもちろん、京都で暮らしているような気分を味わえるのも魅力のひとつ。

Guests talking happily in a communal area

オープンスペースでは宿泊客同士が楽しげに会話を交わす姿も見られる。

Most supposedly familiar guesthouses in Kyoto have Japanese-style rooms. Enjoy your Kyoto stay while experiencing cultural differences like walking around your room in bare feet and laying out your *futon*!

おなじみのゲストハウスも、京都なら和室がほとんど。裸足で部屋の中を歩きまわったり、ふとんを敷いたり、文化の違いを感じながら京都ステイを楽しんで!

This is a typical dormitory room. When you want to lie down, lay out your futon. Fold up your *futon* as in the photo when you are not using it.

ドミトリーの一室。布団は横になりたい時に自分で敷こう。使わない時は写真のようにたたむのがマナー。

The basic rule is that you do your own cooking, cleaning up and washing. Rules differ depending on the guesthouse so listen carefully when you check in.

食事の準備や後片付け、洗濯は自分でするのが基本。ゲストハウスによって館内のルールが違うので、チェックイン時にしっかり説明を受けよう。

Kyoto has many narrow and one-way streets so bicycles are a convenient means of transport. Some guesthouses lend out bicycles so you can use these to roam around the area.

狭い路地や一方通行の道が多い京都では、自転車が便利な交通手段。自転車の貸し出しをしているゲストハウスもあるのでまわりをサイクリングするのもいいだろう。

Gojō Guesthouse
五条ゲストハウス

A guesthouse rebuilt from an inn. It has a cafe on the 1st floor that serves simple meals.

料理旅館だった建物を改築したゲストハウス。1Fには簡単な食事を取れるカフェスペースがある。

Search for a guesthouse here! You can search for guesthouses around the world

ゲストハウスはここで検索!世界中のゲストハウスが探せる。

http://www.hostelworld.com

MAP　P105E-1
東山区五条橋東3丁目396-2
5 min walk from Keihan Gojō Station
¥ 2500 (per person, separate dormitories for men and women), ¥ 6000 (2 people, twin room)
http://www.gojo-guest-house.com/　※ Make bookings by e-mail from the guesthouse website

Manners and etiquette

Prohibitions on photography

撮影禁止

Photography within shrines and temples requires particular caution. Basically, you should think that photography of things designated as world cultural heritage or national treasure such as Buddha statues and buildings is prohibited. Furthermore, some places do not permit the use of tripods even if they allow photography. Also, do not take photos at cinemas, art galleries or museums either.

社寺内での撮影は特に注意。仏像や建物など、世界文化遺産や国宝の指定を受けているものは基本的に撮影禁止と考えた方がいい。また、撮影は許可されていても、三脚の使用が不可の場所もある。映画館、美術館、博物館もNG。

Prohibitions on shoes

土足厳禁

The general rule in Japan is to take your shoes off when going inside. Take care because in addition to Japanese inns, you may even have to take your shoes off at some restaurants, etc. Take care at places where there is a step at the entrance or at a corridor proceeding to a room. Check to see if other people have left their shoes or if there are any shoe lockers. In particular, if you are going into the main hall of a temple, make sure to take off your shoes.

日本では、室内に上がる時は靴を脱ぐのが一般的。旅館はもちろん、お店でも靴を脱がなければならないところがある。特に、お寺の本堂に入る場合は、必ず靴を脱がなくてはならない。

People tend to get very excited when they go on holiday. Going overseas in particular involves cultural differences and if you do make some kind of mistake it can even ruin your long-awaited holiday. Remember this short guide to manners and etiquette and be a smart traveler.

旅先ではついついはしゃいでしまうもの。特に海外だと文化の違いもある。事前にマナーを知って、スマートな旅行者になろう。

Prohibitions on eating and drinking

飲食禁止

Because there are so many delicious things to eat in Kyoto, there are many stores where you can get takeaway food. However, just because you bought something somewhere, it does not necessarily mean that you can eat it anywhere!

おいしいものが揃う京都には、テイクアウトできる店も多数。だからと言って、そこら中で食べてもいいわけではない。

Gardens
庭園

The beautifully managed gardens at temples and other gardens made by landscape gardeners are valued as cultural property so food and drink that may mess them up are forbidden.

美しく管理されたお寺の庭や庭師が調えた庭は文化財として価値があるので、それを汚す可能性のある飲食はだめ。

Buses and trains
バス・電車

Eating and drinking on trains may not necessarily be prohibited, but if you spill or drop things, you may inconvenience other passengers so avoid eating and drinking on trains.

禁止されてはいないが、他の乗客に迷惑がかかる恐れがあるので、できるだけ避けよう。

In front of convenience stores
コンビニの前

Eating and drinking in front of convenience stores is not prohibited, but avoid doing so from a moral perspective.

禁止されてはいないが、モラルとして避けよう。

Points to remember about toilets
トイレの注意点

Toilets at stations and in parks, etc, are basically free.Some toilets do not have toilet paper so carry some with you.Sometimes you can use the toilet at a convenience store.

駅や公園などのトイレは基本的に無料。トイレットペーパーがないトイレもあるので、紙は持参しよう。コンビニで借りられることもある。

Trilingual Kyoto dialect

English／英語	Japanese／日本語	Kyō kotoba／京ことば
Welcome	irasshai mase いらっしゃいませ	oideyasu/okoshiyasu おいでやす・おこしやす
Thank you	arigatō ありがとう	ōkini おおきに
Thanks for everything	itsumo arigatō いつもありがとう	maido まいど
You can't do that!	dame だめ	akan あかん
Keep it up!	ganbatte がんばって	okibari yasu おきばりやす
Thank you for having me	ojama shimashita お邪魔しました	oyakamassan doshita おやかまっさんどした
How cute!	kawaiine かわいいね	kairashinà かいらしなぁ
Sorry	gomen nasai ごめんなさい	kannin dosue 堪忍どすえ
No problem	mondai nai 問題ない	daiji ohen 大事おへん
That is troublesome, isn't it?	komatta koto desune 困ったことですね	nangina koccha 難儀なこっちゃ

Did something happen?	nanika attano desuka 何かあったのですか	nannzo oshitanka なんぞおしたんか
Thanks for your trouble	gokurōsama ご苦労様	habakarisan はばかりさん
You're welcome/ Far from it	tondemonai とんでもない	messomonai めっそもない
To go north	kita e iku 北へ行く	agaru 上がる
To go south	minami e iku 南へ行く	sagaru 下がる
A first-time / walk-in customer	shotaimen no kyaku/ tobikomi no kyaku 初対面の客・飛び込みの客	ichigenhan 一見はん
Mess around	fuzakeru ふざける	ichibiru いちびる
Malicious	iji ga warui 意地が悪い	ikezu いけず
Sophisticated brightness	jōhinna akarusa 上品な明るさ	hannari はんなり
Somehow / other	nantoka なんとか	bochibochi ぼちぼち
Feel relief	hotto suru ほっとする	hokkori suru ほっこりする
A lot	takusan たくさん	yōke よーけ

Word Bank

観光
Sightseeing

ここはどこですか？
Where am I?

【平安神宮】へ行く道を
教えてください
Could you tell me how I get
to 【Heian-jingū】?

歩いて何分くらい
かかりますか？
How long does it take if I
walk?

トイレはどこですか？
Where is a rest room?

写真を撮ってください
Will you take a picture of
us?

食事
Meals

お勧めは何ですか？
What's your recommend?

お勘定をお願いします
Can I have the bill?

大盛りでお願いします
Please give me a large
serving.

激ウマです
This is extremely delicious.

サービス料込みですか？
Is service included in the
bill?

買い物
Shopping

これはいくらですか？
How much is this?

キレイに包んでください
Please wrap it nicely.

高いです
Too expensive.

まけてください
Please give me a discount.

試着していいですか？
Can I try it on?

トラブル
Trouble

具合が悪いです
I don't feel good.

頭が痛いです
I have a headache.

熱があります
I have a fever.

財布を盗まれました
My wallet was stolen.

この近くの病院(交番)は
どこですか？
Where is the nearest hospital (police box)?

Event calendar

Spring 春

3 【March】月

■Average temperature: 7.3℃
　平均気温: 7.3℃
■Average rainfall: 111mm
　平均降水量: 111mm

15th　Seiryō-ji "O-Taimatsu Shiki"　　15日　清凉寺「お松明式」

The O-Taimatsu Shiki is one of the 3 great fire festivals of Kyoto. 3 pine torches set up are set alight in the evening. The priests divine the abundance or paucity of the year, harvest from the vitality of the flames.

涅槃会法要の後に行われる、京都に春の訪れを告げる行事。京都三大火祭として受け継がれ、当日夜に境内に立てられた3基の大松明を燃やし、炎の勢いによりその年の稲作の豊凶を占う。

Mid-March　Higashiyama area "Kyoto-Higashiyama Hanatōro"　　中旬　東山地域「京都・東山花灯路」

As many as 2400 lanterns and *ikebana* flower arrangements give fantastic colour to a walkway from Shōren-in in the north through Maruyama Park and Yasaka-jinja to Kiyomizu-dera in the south. Shrines and temples in the area also make special visiting arrangements during the event.

北は青蓮院から円山公園、八坂神社を抜けて南の清水寺までの散策路を約2400基の行灯のライトアップといけばなが飾る。周辺社寺での特別拝観も行われる。

4 【April】月

■Average temperature: 15.1℃
　平均気温: 15.1℃
■Average rainfall: 188mm
　平均降水量: 188mm

Late-March to mid-April　Nijō-jō "Light-up"　　3月下旬～4月中旬　二条城「ライトアップ」

During the event, the blossoms of the roughly 200 wild cherry, Sato-zakura and weeping cherry trees in the castle grounds are lit up gorgeously. You can observe flower arrangement and Japanese music in the kitchen of the Ninomaru Goten.

城内に咲く約200本の桜や庭園がライトアップされる。特別公開される重要文化財の二の丸御殿の台所では、華道や邦楽などを鑑賞できる。

10th　Hirano-jinja "Ōkasai"　　10日　平野神社「桜花祭」

This festival is for admiring cherry blossoms and is said to have started following an imperial decree. This shrine is famous for its cherry trees. There are about 400 cherry trees of 50 varieties. You can also enjoy evening cherry blossom viewing until the middle of April.

天皇の勅令により始まったとされる桜を愛でる祭。平野神社は50種約400本もの桜が咲き誇る桜の名所。4月半ばまで夜桜見物も楽しめる。

1st to 30th　Gion Kōbu Kaburen-jō Theater "Miyako Odori"
1～30日　祇園甲部歌舞練場「都をどり」

The Miyako Odori is a dance performance with a history of more than 130 years. *Geiko* and *maiko* perform traditional Kyoto dances. The repertoire is derived from *kabuki* and famous stories such as *Genji Monogatari* and continues to change with a new orientation each year.

130年以上の歴史ある都をどりは京都の花街・祇園甲部の芸妓や舞妓が京舞などを披露する。演目は歌舞伎や源氏物語などを題材にして、毎年新たな趣向で上演され続けている。

5 【May】月

■Average temperature: 19.6℃
　平均気温: 19.6℃
■Average rainfall: 118.5mm
　平均降水量: 118.5mm

15th　Shimogamo-jinja/ Kamigamo-jinja "Aoi Festival"　　15日　下鴨神社・上賀茂神社「葵祭」

The Aoi Festival is one of the three great festivals of Kyoto.This festival takes place at the Shimogamo-jinja and Kamigamo-jinja. About 500 participants wearing Heian Period costumes form a procession about 700m long. They make their way from the Kyoto Gosho through Shimogamo-jinja to the Kamigamo-jinja.

葵祭は京都三大祭のひとつで、下鴨神社と上賀茂神社で行われる。平安装束の約500名、全長700mもの行列が京都御所から下鴨神社を経由して上賀茂神社まで向かう。

15th　Shimogamo-jinja "Yabusame and Busha Shintō rituals"　　15日　下鴨神社「流鏑馬と歩射神事」

The Yabusame and Busha Shintō rituals are carried out as pre-rituals for the Aoi Festival in the Tadasu-no-mori forest within the Shimogamo-jinja.In the Yabusame ritual, horse riders fire arrows at targets while they ride and in the Busha ritual, archers fire arrows while walking on the ground.

葵祭の前儀として、下鴨神社境内の糺の森で行われる。流鏑馬神事は馬上から騎手が矢で的を射抜いていく。歩射神事は射手が歩きながら矢を射って葵祭の沿道を清める。

3rd Sunday of May　Kurumazaki-jinja "Mifune Festival"　　第3日曜　車折神社「三船祭」

The Mifune Festival reenacts the boat games of the Heian Period. 20 colourful boats are floated on the Ōi river that flows through Arashiyama.

嵐山を流れる大堰川に御座船や龍頭船など装飾の華やかな船20数隻を浮かべて、平安時代の船遊びを再現する。京都の初夏を代表する風物詩のひとつだ。

【June】

6月

■Average temperature: 22.7℃
平均気温：22.7℃
■Average rainfall: 262mm
平均降水量：262mm

1st & 2nd   Heian-jingū "Takigi Nō"   1・2日   平安神宮「薪能」

The Takigi *Nō* drama performances start at sunset. Fires are lit in front of the shrine hall where superb actors play opposite each other. Various types of play are performed on the stage.

夕暮れ時に始まる能楽舞台。社殿の前に火が焚かれ、優れた演者の競演が行われる。舞台ではさまざまな種類の演目が繰り広げられる。

30th   Kamigamo-jinja "Minazuki Ōharae Shiki"
30日   上賀茂神社「水無月大祓式」

This is a ritual for making prayers so that people can purify the sins and impurities of the first half of the year and spend the summer safely. Participants first of all pass through a ring made of cogon grass and conduct the purification ritual in a wooden hashidono structure built over a stream. Then the Nagoshi ritual is carried out to clear away the sins they have committed and their impurities.

半年間の罪・けがれを祓い、夏を無事に過ごせるよう祈願する行事。まず参加者は茅の輪をくぐり、橋殿で祓の儀式を行う。その後、犯した罪やけがれを除き去るための夏越神事が行われる。

【July】

7月

■Average temperature: 24.3℃
平均気温：24.3℃
■Average rainfall: 256mm
平均降水量：256mm

1st to 31st   Yasaka-jinja "Gion Festival"   1〜31日   八坂神社「祇園祭」

The Gion Festival is a traditional summer festival held through July to drive away pestilence. A parade of 32 *yamaboko* floats is held around the city on the 17th.

祇園祭は疫病退散を願って7月を通して行われる、伝統の夏祭り。17日には32基の山鉾が市内を巡行する山鉾巡行が行わる。文化財である山鉾が公道をめぐるため「動く美術館」とも言われる。

27th to 30th   Shimogamo-jinja "Mitarashi Festival"
27〜30日   下鴨神社「御手洗祭」

The Mitarashi Festival holds at the Mitarashi-jinja enshrined in the Mitarashi Lake in the Shimogamo-jinja. People wade into the lake to shrug off their sins and impurities. This lake is also said to be effective for illness and safe childbirth.

下鴨神社境内の御手洗池に祀られている御手洗神社で足つけ神事が行われる。この池の中に足を浸すと、罪やけがれが取り除かれるとされる。また、病気や安産にも効き目があるといわれている。

【August】

8月

■Average temperature: 27.6℃
平均気温：27.6℃
■Average rainfall: 298.5mm
平均降水量：298.5mm

9th   Mibu-dera "Mibu Rokusai Nenbutsu"
9日   壬生寺「壬生六斎念仏」

The Rokusai Nenbutsu is a folk ritual. People dance to bells and drums while reciting the Buddhist nenbutsu chant. At Mibu-dera, the Rokusai Nenbutsu is held from about 8pm, in combination with a memorial service for ancestral spirits. There are also *shishimai* acrobats and confrontations with spiders.

壬生寺では、鉦や太鼓ではやし、念仏を唱えながら踊る六斎念仏を先祖の霊を供養する行事とあわせて20時頃から行う。獅子舞や蜘蛛との対決等の派手な芸が見もの。

16th   Kyoto City "Gozan Okuribi"   16日   京都市内「五山送り火」

This is a seasonal tradition that lights up the summer night sky. It is held to see off the spirits heading back to the netherworld following the Obon Festival of the Dead. First of all, the Japanese character "dai" meaning "big" is lit on Higashiyama Nyoigatake Mountain. Then, the characters "myō" and "hō", a boat shaped pattern, and again the character "dai" appear in fire on other mountains. Lastly, the shape of a *torii* shrine gate appears to give a total of 6 characters and symbols rising up in flames on the mountains around the city.

夏の夜空を彩るこの風物詩は、冥府に帰る精霊を送るためのもの。最初に東山如意ヶ嶽の「大文字」が点火され、「妙」「法」「船形」「左大文字」、最後に「鳥居形」と6つの文字・記号が炎によって浮かび上がる。

【September】

9月

■Average temperature: 25℃
平均気温：25℃
■Average rainfall: 137.5mm
平均降水量：137.5mm

July 1st to September 15th Arashiyama/ Ōi river "Ukai"   7月1日～9月15日 嵐山・大堰川「鵜飼い」

Ukai is an ancient method of fishing. Cormorants are domesticated and trained to catch fish such as sweetfish. Ukai takes place on nights from July to mid-September. The fishermen keep fires in their boats as they float on the river. You can watch from a different boat. ※ A charge must be paid to board a viewing boat

鵜飼いとは、鵜を飼いならしてアユなどの魚を捕らせる古くからの漁法で毎年7月～9月中旬の夜に行われる。別の船から見物できる。※乗船料必要

9th Kamigamo-jinja "Karasu-zumō"   9日 上賀茂神社「烏相撲」

This is a *sumō* event to get rid of evil spirits. Two people carrying bows and arrows jump about sideways as though dancing like birds. They also cry out 'kā kā kā' to mimic the cries of birds. After that, children wearing loincloths do *sumō*.

ふたりの人物が弓矢を持ち、烏が踊るように横跳びをしたり、「カーカーカー」と鳴きまねをしたりする。その後、子供たちが元気よく相撲を取る。

【October】

10月

■Average temperature: 16.9℃
平均気温：16.9℃
■Average rainfall: 53mm
平均降水量：53mm

1st to 5th Kitano Tenman-gū "Zuiki Festival"   1～5日 北野天満宮「ずいき祭」

The roof of the Zuiki *mikoshi* portable shrine used in The Zuiki festival is made using taro stalks and the shrine as a whole is draped with dried products such as vegetables and *yuba* bean curd skin.

祭では、ずいき（さといもの茎）で屋根を作り、野菜や湯葉などの乾物で覆った「ずいきみこし」が登場する。

22nd Kyoto Gosho to Heian-jingū "Jidai Festival"   22日 京都御所～平安神宮「時代祭」

The Jidai Festival takes place looking back over the 8 eras when the capital was located in Kyoto. A procession about 2km long of about 2000 people dressed in the costumes of each age walks along a roughly 4.5km course from Kyoto Gosho to Heian-Jingū.

京都に都が置かれた8つの時代を遡って行列を行う。御所から平安神宮までの約4.5kmのコースを、総勢約2000名、総延長2kmにも及ぶ各時代の装束を身につけた行列が歩く。

22nd Yuki-jinja "Kurama Fire Festival"   22日 由岐神社「鞍馬の火祭」

The Kurama Fire Festival is one of the 3 great festivals of Kyoto. Fires are lit all at once from 6pm at the signal of the ritual manager. While calling out "sairei sairyō" means festival, young people walk along in procession carrying flaming torches.

京都三大奇祭のひとつで、祭神を御所から由岐神社に迎えた模様を伝える祭。18時から「神事振れ」の合図で一斉に点火された大松明を「サイレイ、サイリョウ（＝祭礼）」と声を掛けながら、抱えて練り歩く。

【November】

11月

■Average temperature: 14.4℃
平均気温：14.4℃
■Average rainfall: 75.2mm
平均降水量：75.2mm

3rd Jōnan-gū "Kyokusui no Utage"   3日 城南宮「曲水の宴（きょくすいのうたげ）」

The Kyokusui no Utage festival takes place in the Jōnan-gū garden. The festival reenacts a game played by the Heian Period aristocracy. 7 singers dressed in the Heian Period make *waka* poems using themes that float down from upstream on trays.

平安貴族の遊びを再現した行事。平安装束に身を包んだ7名の歌人が庭園の小川沿いの席に座り、川上から盆に乗って流れてくる題目の和歌を詠む。

Late October to early December Kōdai-ji "Special nighttime opening in autumn"   10月下旬～12月上旬 高台寺「秋の夜間特別拝観」

After sunset, the temple lights up the beautiful autumn colours of the trees in its gardens, and around its lake and bamboo grove. The visiting hours of the temple are extended especially. An elaborate arrangement is also set up in the Hojo Garden.

期間中の夜間は、紅葉の美しい境内の庭園などのライトアップや夜間拝観が行われる。方丈の庭は趣向を凝らした設えで、境内庭園とはひと味違った夜景が楽しめる。

Winter 冬

【December】

12月

■Average temperature:7.2℃
平均気温:7.2℃
■Average rainfall: 36.5mm
平均降水量:36.5mm

Mid-December　Saga/ Arashiyama area "Kyoto-Arashiyama Hanatôro"　中旬　嵯峨・嵐山地域「京都・嵐山花灯路」

Starting with the Togetsu-kyô area, paths through bamboo groves and surrounding temples, shrines and cultural facilities are lit up. Several special opening events are held at shrines, temples and other places.

渡月橋周辺を始め、竹林の小径や周辺寺院・神社・文化施設がライトアップされ、特別拝観・開館や数々のイベントが行われる。

31st　Yasaka-jinja "Okera Mairi"　31日　八坂神社「をけら詣り」

The Okera Mairi is a New Year's Eve event held to see out the year. Shintô ritual fires are lit in 2 lanterns set inside the shrine precincts. Visitors transfer this fire to pieces of bamboo rope and keep swinging the ropes around to keep the embers hot while they make their way home. It is said that if you use these embers to start the fire to prepare your New Year cuisine, you will pass the whole year in sound health.

一年の最後の日・大晦日に行われる年越し行事。境内の灯籠に神事の火が灯され、参拝者はこの火を縄に移して回転させながら家に持ち帰る。新年を迎える料理などの火種としてこれを使うと、一年間無病息災で過ごせると言われる。

【January】

1月

■Average temperature:3.9℃
平均気温:3.9℃
■Average rainfall: 97.5mm
平均降水量:97.5mm

4th　Shimogamo-jinja "Kemari Hajime"　4日　下鴨神社「蹴鞠初め」

Kemari was enjoyed by Heian Period aristocrats. On the day of the *Kemari* Hajime event, members of the *Kemari* Preservation Society dressed in the Heian Period play *kemari*.

蹴鞠とは平安時代に貴族たちが楽しんだもの。当日は、平安貴族の装束を身につけた蹴鞠保存会の人たちが、掛け声を掛けながら鞠を蹴り上げて遊ぶ様子を見物できる。

3rd　Yasaka-jinja "Karuta Hajime Shiki"　3日　八坂神社「かるた始め式」

Girls dressed in beautiful 12-layered ceremonial kimono play *karuta*, exhibiting their prowess at sending the right card flying when a performer recites the *waka* poem written upon it.

十二単姿の女性たちによる鮮やかにかるたの札を飛ばす妙技が披露される。

【February】

2月

■Average temperature:5.5℃
平均気温:5.5℃
■Average rainfall: 64mm
平均降水量:64mm

3rd　Heian-jingû "Setsubun Festival"　3日　平安神宮「節分祭」

February 3 is Setsubun, the day when the season turns from winter to spring. In Japan there is a custom on this day of conducting rituals to drive away pestilence and invite good fortune. The Heian-jingû Setsubun Festival reenacts the purification ritual inside the shrine. The priests throw beans at bad spirits to drive them away, making a tremendous impact.

冬から春への変わり目に当たる節分には、悪疫を退散して福を招く行事を行う風習がある。平安神宮では悪い鬼に豆を投げて追い払う行事が行われる。

Late February　Kamigamo-jinja "Nentô Festival"　下旬　上賀茂神社「燃灯祭」

The people of the Heian Period used to go and play in the fields picking young greens. This festival has ritualized such activities. On the day of the festival, you can go along with the festival performers and watch as they offer plants before the altar.

平安時代の人が春を待ちこがれて野原で若菜を摘んだという野辺遊びを行事化したもの。当日は、祭官達が草木を神前に献上するのを見学できる。

25th　Kitano Tenman-gû "Baika Festival"　25日　北野天満宮「梅花祭」

The god of wisdom, Sugawara no Michizane, is worshipped at the Kitano Tenman-gû. From about early February to late March, about 20000 plum trees of 50 varieties blossom in the shrine's expansive precincts of roughly 66000 m². Apart from Shintô rituals, *geiko* and *maiko* from Kamishichiken hold an open air tea ceremony during the Baika Festival. (There is a charge for the tea ceremony)

学問の神様・菅原道真公が祀られる神社で、2月上旬〜3月下旬頃には境内の梅50種約2000本が咲き誇る。梅花祭では神事のほか、上七軒の芸妓や舞妓達による野点茶会も行われる(茶会は料金必要)。

The neighboring guides of Kyoto Station

京都駅周辺ガイド

SPOT1 Best views
ベストビュー

Grand Staircase, Sky Plaza, Skyway
大階段・大空広場・空中径路

The Grand Staircase is on the western side of the Kyoto Station Building, has a total of 171 steps, and rises 30 m. The Sky Plaza is on the roof after you ascend the Grand Staircase. The splendid views from this location are the best in the station building. You can see Kyoto Tower from the glass-paneled Skyway on the 10th floor. The view at night is fantastic!

京都駅ビルの西側にある全171段、高低差30mの大階段。この階段を上った屋上には大空広場があり、その見晴らしのよさは駅ビル内で一番。また、10階のガラス張りの通路・空中径路は目前に京都タワーを望め、夜景も最高！

SPOT2 Sentō
銭湯

Kyoto Tower Daiyokujō bathhouse
京都タワー タワー大浴場

This bathhouse with saunas is on the 3rd underground floor of Kyoto Tower that is opposite Kyoto station building. The baths are spacious and you can relax and remove the fatigue of your trip. The Daiyokujō is open from early in the morning. ¥750

京都駅ビル向かいの、京都タワー地下3階にあるサウナつきの銭湯。広々とした造りで、ゆったりと旅の疲れを癒せる。早朝から営業している。¥750

This way with 45m above the ground is connected to Hotel Granvia Kyoto. You can feel like walking in the sky. Also, you can see Kyoto Tower in front of you.

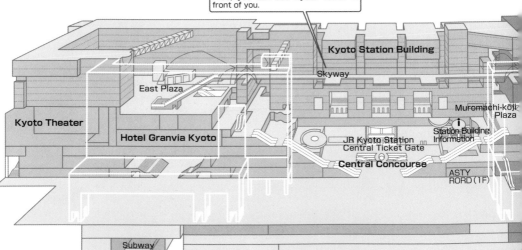

Kyoto Station is the entranceway to Kyoto. Apart from a hotel, the station building contains a theater, restaurants and shops. We recommend the use of these facilities for the start and end of your visit.

京都の玄関口である京都駅。駅ビルにはホテルのほか劇場、レストランやショッピング施設も充実しているので、ぜひ活用しよう。

SPOT3 Large-scale electronics store
家電量販店

Biccamera, JR Kyoto Station branch
ビックカメラ JR京都駅店

Biccamera is a large-scale electronics and white goods store that was established on the west side of Kyoto Station in 2007. It is packed with home electronics and appliances including TVs, cameras, audio equipment and PCs and sports equipments. The store also has a direct entrance from Kyoto Station.

2007年に京都駅の西側に開店した家電量販店。テレビ、カメラ、オーディオ、パソコンを始め家電・電化製品のほかにも、スポーツ用品などの豊富な品揃え。JR京都駅と直通の出入口もある。

SPOT4 Bookstore
本屋

Books Sanseidō, Kyoto Station branch
三省堂書店 京都駅店

Books Sanseidō is a bookshop in The CUBE, the shopping arcade on the underground floor of the Kyoto Station Building. Books Sanseidō sells maps, guidebooks, photographic album of Kyoto and Japanese Manga. Sanseidō also has foreign-language books.

京都駅ビルの地下にある専門店街The CUBE内にある本屋。地図や観光ガイドはもちろん、京都の写真集やコミックが充実している。洋書もある。

The youth often talk with their friends on the Grand Staircase with 171 steps. Live broadcasting and events are sometimes performed. The night view from the rooftop is more romantic.

Sky Plaza (happi-terrace)

Grand Staircase

JR Kyoto Isetan Department Store

Parking

Specialty Store Street The CUBE (B2~1F,11F)

This department store sells good souvenirs and you should check delis at the basement. Why don't you have a picnic with a box lunch looked by the long-established restaurant?

A quick bus guide

Many sightseeing spots in Kyoto are closest to bus stops so moving around by bus is convenient. However, Kyoto has many bus types and routes and it is difficult even for locals to understand them all. You should try to remember just the combination of your main destination and route. When you transfer from the train to the bus at Kyoto Station, first of all, go to the Bus Information Center. At the center, you can buy things such as cards for riding on Kyoto city buses.

観光スポットめぐりはバスでの移動が便利。しかし、路線数が多く、すべてを理解するのは地元民でも難しい。まずはバス総合案内所へ立ち寄ろう。京都市バスの乗車カードなどが購入可能。

Bus stops in front of Kyoto Station
京都駅前バスのりば

The bus terminal at Kyoto Station is in front of the Karasuma Central exit. City buses and buses belonging to Kyoto Bus, JR Bus, Keihan Bus and other lines depart and arrive from here.

京都駅のバスターミナルは烏丸中央口前にある。ここから市バス・京都バス・JRバス・京阪バスなどのバスが発着している。

Special value tickets
お得な乗車券

If you want to spend a day visiting various sightseeing spots around Kyoto, it is way better value to use a day ticket for unlimited travel. You can buy these cards at the Bus Information Center in front of Kyoto Station so buy one first thing if you visit Kyoto.

あちこち観光してまわるなら、乗り降り自由の一日乗車券などを利用するのが断然お得。京都駅前のバス総合案内所などで購入できる。

Ticket name チケット名	Cost 料金	Zones and routes 乗車可能な区間・路線	Advice アドバイス
Kyoto Sightseeing All-day Pass Card 京都観光一日乗車券	¥1200 (2days ¥2000)	・All Kyoto subway lines ・All city bus routes ・Designated Kyoto Bus zones ・京都市営地下鉄全線 ・市バス全線 ・京都バスの指定区間	You can also get a guidebook with special offers such as preferential tickets for visiting temples and shrines, and discount tickets for using facilities 社寺の参拝優遇券や施設利用割引券などの特典つきガイドマップがもらえる
City Bus All day Pass 市バス専用一日乗車券カード	¥500	・City bus uniform fare zone. ・Rakubus ・市バスの均一区間 ・洛バス	You can get a city bus route map when you buy a this ticket at the Bus Information Center. 案内所で購入すると市バスルートマップがもらえる

Bus Information Center - Kyoto Ekimae Information Center
バス総合案内所 京都駅前案内所

Exit through the Karasuma Central ticket barrier and the center is on the right hand side. Beyond the Information Center are some small coin lockers. If you are making a day trip starting and finishing at Kyoto Station, you can leave anything you do not need here.

京都駅の烏丸中央改札を出て右手にある。案内所奥には小型のコインロッカーが少しある。

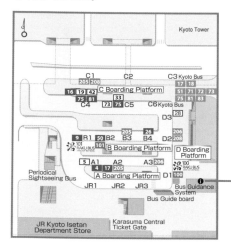

Get the map!

You can get a city bus route map when you buy a bus ticket at the Bus Information Center. Make sure to get a map before you get on the bus!

バス総合案内所では、乗車券を購入すると市バスの路線マップをもらえる。

Bus Information Center
Kyoto Ekimae Information Center
バス総合案内所 京都駅前案内所
☎075-371-4474
7:30〜20:00

Caution! 注意!	You can visit these places! ここへ行ける!	
	City Bus All-day Pass zone+Arashiyama, Sagano, Ōhara, Shūgakuin and Takao. 市バス専用一日乗車券カードの範囲+嵐山・嵯峨野・大原・修学院・高雄方面	京都観光一日乗車券 One Day Pass
You cannot use this ticket for buses going to Arashiyama, Sagano, Ōhara, Shūgakuin, or Takao. You have to pay a separate charge! 嵐山・嵯峨野・大原・修学院・高雄方面へのバスは別運賃が必要!	Kinkaku-ji, Ginkaku-ji, Kiyomizu-dera, Nijō-jō, Ryōan-ji, Kyoto Gyoen, Daitoku-ji, Tōfuku-ji and Fushimi Inari Taisha, etc. 金閣寺・銀閣寺・清水寺・二条城・龍安寺・京都御苑・大徳寺・東福寺・伏見稲荷大社など	市バス専用 一日乗車券カード 500円

Let's ride the bus!

City buses and Kyoto bus

市バスと京都バス

City buses
市バス

City buses are the yellow-green ones you see most often in Kyoto. City buses cover the whole city from their terminal in front of Kyoto Station.

最も多く目にする黄緑色の車体のバス。京都駅前のターミナルを起点に、市内全域をカバー。

Rakubus
洛バス

The Rakubus is a type of city bus and runs express routes linking famous sightseeing spots around Kyoto. You can travel to locations such as Kinkaku-ji, Ginkaku-ji, and Kiyomizu-dera. (Refer to p4-7 for details.)

市バスの一種で、市内の観光名所を結ぶ急行バス。P4〜7参照。

Kyoto Bus
京都バス

Kyoto Buses are convenient for transfers to Arashiyama and Sagano in the west, and Ōhara and Hiei-zan in the north from bases in front of Kyoto Station, Sanjō Keihan Station and elsewhere.

京都駅前、三条京阪前などを起点に西部の嵐山・嵯峨野方面、北部の大原・比叡山方面への移動に便利。

Route numbers and fares

系統番号と運賃

Different city buses travel to the same destinations via different routes so you can travel with more certainty if you remember the route numbers. Route numbers are displayed in destination display windows on the fronts of buses.

市バスは同じ目的地でも経由が異なるバスがあるので、路線番号を覚えておくといい。

Blue × White 9

Buses with numbers printed in outline on a blue background run standard routes in a uniform fare zone. One ride costs ¥220.

青地に白抜きの番号は、均一運賃区間を走る系統のバスで一乗車220円。

Orange × White 201

Buses with numbers printed in outline on an orange background run circular routes in a uniform fare zone. Numbers range from 201 to 208.

オレンジ地に白抜きの番号は、均一運賃区間を走る循環系統のバス。系統番号は201〜208。

White × Black 69

Buses with black numbers on a white background charge variable fares according to the distance travelled. Take a numbered zone ticket when you get on and pay the fare shown for that zone number when you get off.

白地に黒文字の番号は、走行距離で運賃が変動するバス。乗車時に整理券を取り、降車時に整理券番号に応じた運賃を支払う。

Pale blue × White 100

Buses with numbers printed in outline on a pale blue background run sightseeing routes in a uniform fare zone. Numbers are 100, 101 and 102.

水色地に白抜きの番号は、均一運賃区間を走る洛バス。系統番号は100・101・102の3系統。

Lets! Go by Bus
How to use buses   バスの乗り方

A city bus has one operator. Board from the rear door and alight from the front. Put the fare in the fare box when you alight.

市バスは後ろのドアから乗車し、前のドアから降車するワンマンカー。運賃は降車時に運賃箱に入れよう。

1 Look for your bus stop
バス停を探す

Look for a bus stop consisting of a light blue sign with "City Bus" written on it. The main bus stops operate on a system that announces the approach of a bus by radio.
※ Please be careful as there can be multiple bus stops with the same name but for different destinations and routes.

水色の看板で、「市バス」と書かれた停留所を探そう。また主要なバス停では、無線でバスの接近を知らせるシステムがある。

☑ Confirm your destination
行き先を確認する

When a bus for the route (destination) indicated on the bus stop approaches, check the destination and number in the display window of the front of the bus.

バス前方の行き先表示欄の目的地・系統番号を確認しよう。

☑ Board the bus from the rear door
後ろのドアから乗車する

Board the bus from the rear door. If the zone ticket machine prints a ticket when you board, do not forget to take it (if you are using a travel card, make sure to run the card through the card machine).

区間料金制のバスは整理券を取り忘れないように(乗車カード利用の場合は、必ずカード専用の機械にカードを通すこと)。

☑ Press the button before your destination
目的地の前でボタンを押す

Check the announcements and display for your bus stop and press the drop off button early.

下車するバス停のアナウンスや表示を確認して、早めに降車ボタンを押そう。

☑ Pay the fare and alight
運賃を支払って降車する

Prepare small change, a ticket-book or your travel card and pay your fare after the bus stops. Alight from the front door. Put coins in the fare box and either pass a card through the card machine or present it to the driver.

小銭・カード乗車券・回数券を用意し、バスが停車してから運賃を支払い、前のドアから降車する。小銭は運賃箱に、カードは専用のカードに通す運転手に掲示する。

Changing money
両替方法

If paying by ¥500 coin or ¥1000 note, change these to smaller coins using the change machine beneath the fare box before you get off. You cannot change ¥2000, ¥5000 or ¥10000 notes on board so make sure to change them before you get on.

500円硬貨・1000円札で支払う場合は、降車前に運賃箱下の両替機で小銭に両替をしよう。また2000円札・5000円札・10000円札を車内で両替することはできないので、必ず乗車前に両替を済ませよう。

Caution! 注意!

When riding on a bus in a uniform fare zone
均一区間バスに乗車する時

If paying by cash, ticket-book ticket, or card, put your coins or ticket in the fare box. The fare is ¥220 for adults and ¥110 for children. (The ¥100 circular route bus that runs only in the central area of the city is ¥100 for both adults and children.)

現金・回数券・カードで乗車する場合は、運賃箱に小銭または回数券を入れ、カードは運転手に見せる。運賃は、大人220円・小児110円(市内中心部のみ走る100円循環バスもある)。

When using a multi-zone bus
区間バスに乗車する時

If paying by cash or ticket-book ticket, check the fare displayed on the display at the front of the bus for your zone ticket number, and put your coins or ticket in the fare box along with the zone ticket. ※If you do not have a zone ticket, your fare will be calculated from the bus' station of origin so care is required.

現金・回数券で乗車する場合は、整理券番号とバス前方掲示板に表示された運賃を確認し、小銭または回数券と整理券を一緒に運賃箱に入れる。※整理券を持っていない場合は、始発からの運賃となるので要注意。

Recommended ways to move around Kyoto

Rickshaw
人力車

Like today's taxis, the rickshaw was a mainstream means of transport from the Meiji to Taishō eras. At present, rickshaw operators will take you around the main sightseeing spots such as Arashiyama and the Kiyomizu-dera areas while giving you a sightseeing guide. The atmospheric carriage feels surprisingly stable. Being able to see Kyoto from higher up than normal is also appealing.

現在のタクシーのように、明治〜大正時代の主流な交通手段だった人力車。今では、車夫さんがガイドをしながら、嵐山や清水寺エリアなどの主要な観光名所をめぐってくれる。趣のある車体は意外と安定感があり、いつもより高い目線で京都を巡れるのも魅力。

Ebisuya
えびす屋

You can find the rickshaw around Togetsu-kyō or Heian-Jingū and Yasaka-jinja. Prices range from ¥2,000 for 1 person for a 10 minute ride, to ¥3,000~ for 2 people, etc. Consult with the rickshaw operator for times and prices.

嵐山の渡月橋付近や平安神宮・八坂神社近辺で見つけることができる。10分で1人2000円、2人3000円〜など。車夫さんと時間・値段を相談して。

Rent-a-cycle
レンタサイクル

People are often plagued by traffic jams in Kyoto's narrow streets. We recommend a bicycle for traveling around Kyoto smoothly. However, take care not to get so fascinated by the scenery that you neglect your riding! There are shops where you can rent a bicycle in front of stations at the main sightseeing spots and at hotels, etc.

狭い京都の街中では、渋滞に悩まされることもよくある。スムーズに移動するには自転車がお勧め。ただし、風景に見惚れるあまり、運転がおろそかにならないように注意を。主要観光地の駅前、ホテルなどに借りられるお店がある。

Shinpachi Cyaya
新八茶屋
MAP　P110C3
9:00〜17:00(Bicycle can be rent until 16pm)
¥310(1hour)、¥410(2hour)
Shinpachichaya sells ice cream and souvenirs. It is near Togetsu-kyō so it is easy to use.

ソフトクリームやおみやげを販売している店。渡月橋のふもとにあるから利用しやすい。

Yotsuba taxis
四つ葉タクシー

Kyoto's Yotsuba taxis have pictures of 4-leaf clovers painted on the car and light. It is said riding one will bring you luck. Yotsuba taxis were introduced by the Yasaka Taxi Company in 2002. The company is famous for its 3-leaf clover logo. You cannot book a Yotsuba taxi and it is always a mystery where they will appear. Your chances of finding one are 4 in 1400. At that rare level, just being able to ride one will make you feel lucky.

京都には四つ葉のクローバーが車体と行灯に描かれたタクシーが走り、乗れば幸せになれると言われている。四つ葉タクシーは、2002年に三つ葉タクシーで有名なヤサカタクシーが導入したもの。予約不可、出現スポットも謎、遭遇する確率は4/1400台。そのレア度に乗車できただけで、幸せな気分になれる。

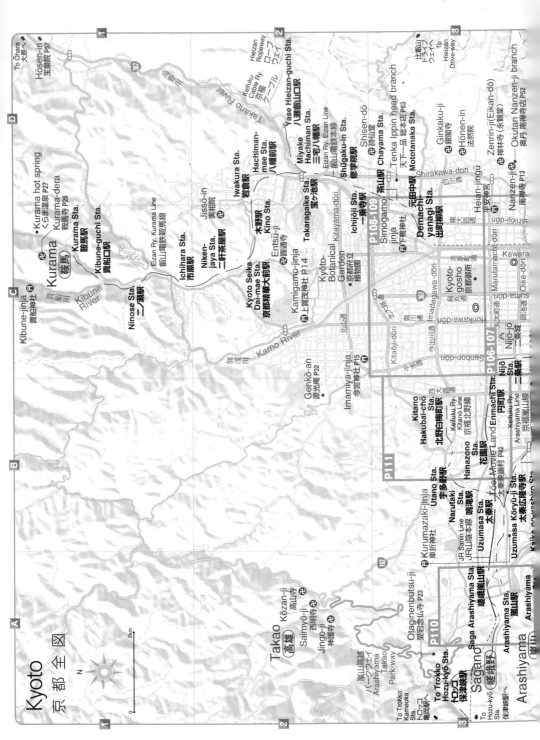

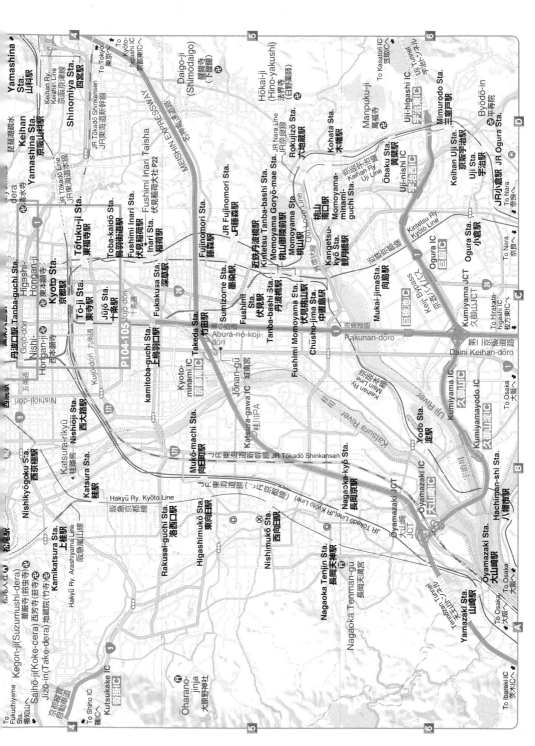

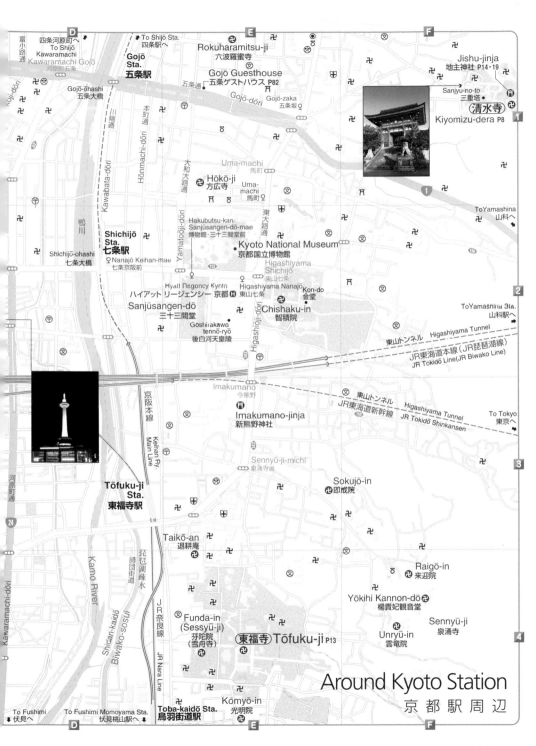

Around Kyoto Station
京都駅周辺

To Saga Arashiyama Sta.
嵯峨嵐山駅へ

To Imadegawa-dōri
今出川通へ

To Imadegawa-dōri
今出川通へ

Horikawa
Marutamachi
堀川丸太町

JR山陰本線（嵯峨野線）

Shinshindō Fuchō-mae branch
進々堂府庁前店

Karasuma
Marutamachi
烏丸丸太町

丸太町通

Marutamachi Sta.
丸太町駅

Nijō-jō
二条城

Seiryū-en
清流園

Kyū-nijō-rikyū
(Nijō-jō)
旧二条離宮

Honmaru
garden
本丸庭園 P29

Ninomaru garden
二の丸庭園

Nijō-jō-mae
二条城前

Ogawa-dōri
小川通

油小路通

Kyoto Kokusai Hotel
京都国際ホテル

ANA Hotel Kyoto
全日空ホテル

Kyoto International
Manga Museum
京都国際
マンガミュージアム P74

地下鉄烏丸線

二条駅
Nijō
Sta.

Subway Tozai Line
地下鉄東西線

Oshikōji-dōri
押小路通

Shinsen-en
神泉苑

二条駅
Nijō
Sta.

二条駅前

Nijō-jō-mae Sta.
二条城前駅

Oike-dōri 御池通

Karasuma Oike
烏丸御池

Karasuma
Oike Sta.
烏丸御池

Horikawa Oike
堀川御池

Kyōto traditional crafts center
京都伝統工芸館

Osteria Ao
オステリア蒼 P72

RAAK
P66

Senbon Sanjō
千本三条

Sanjō-dōri

Horikawa Oike
堀川御池

Mitsui Garden Hotel Kyōto Sanjō
三井ガーデンホテル京都三条

Hyōki
瓢樹

Rokkaku-dō
六角堂 P15

ran Hotei
らん布袋 P55

Abura-no-kōji-dōri

堀川通

大宮通

後院通 Kōin-dōri

JR Sanin Line(Sagano Line)

To Katsura Sta.
桂駅へ

Shijō Horikawa
四条堀川

Shijō Nishi-no-tōin
四条西洞院

Shijō Kyomachiya
四条京町家

Ōmiya Sta.
大宮駅

阪急京都線 Hankyū Ry. Kyōto Line

Keifuku Ry. Arashiyama Line
京福嵐山線

Shijō Ōmiya Sta.
四条大宮駅

Shijō Horikawa
四条堀川

Karasuma Shijō
烏丸四条

Shijō Karasuma
四条烏丸

Shinmachi-dōri

Muromachi-dōri

Subway karasuma Line

東洞院通

室町通

新町通

東横院通

Higashi-no-tōin-dōri

367

嵐山駅へ
To Arashi-
yama Sta.

To Katsura Sta.

Mibu-dera
壬生寺

Yagi-tei
(Shinsen-gumi Mibu-tonsho-ato)
八木邸（新撰組壬生屯所跡）

Yūzen Museum
友禅美術館

Horikawa-dōri

COCON KARASUMA
COCON烏丸

Iisn P65

Karasuma Kyoto Hotel
からすま京都ホテル

Morita Washi
森田和紙 P65

高辻通 Takatsuji-dōri

Byōd
平等寺

Karas
Sta.
烏丸駅

Shijō S
四条駅

Omiya-dōri

Nishi-no-tōin-dōri

Karasuma-dōri

Horikawa Gojō
堀川五条

Karasuma Gojō
烏丸五条

Karasuma Gojō

Kyoto Tokyu Hotel
京都東急ホテル

五条駅
Gojō
Sta.

To Nishi-
kyōgoku
西京極へ

N

中央
卸売市場
Central
Wholesale
Market

Tanba-guchi Sta.
丹波口駅

中央卸売市場
Central
Wholesale
Market

花屋町通

Hanayachō-dōri

24

0   200m

To Kyoto Sta.
京都駅へ

To Nagaoka-kyō
長岡京へ

To Kyoto Sta.
京都駅へ

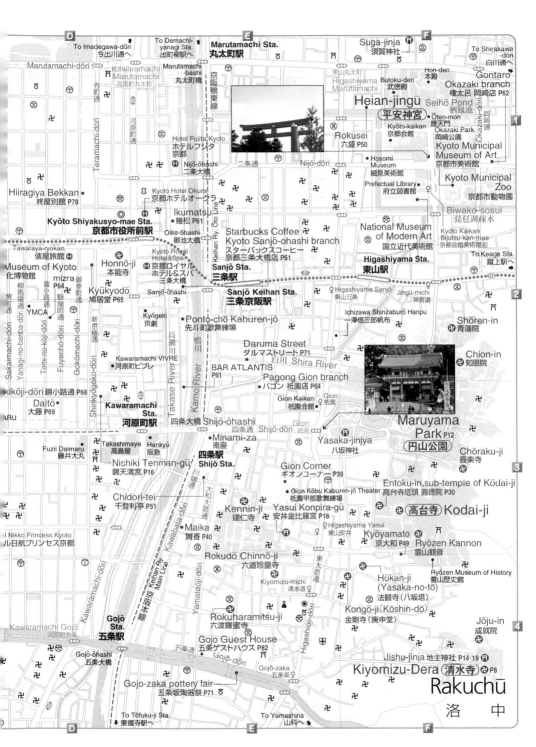

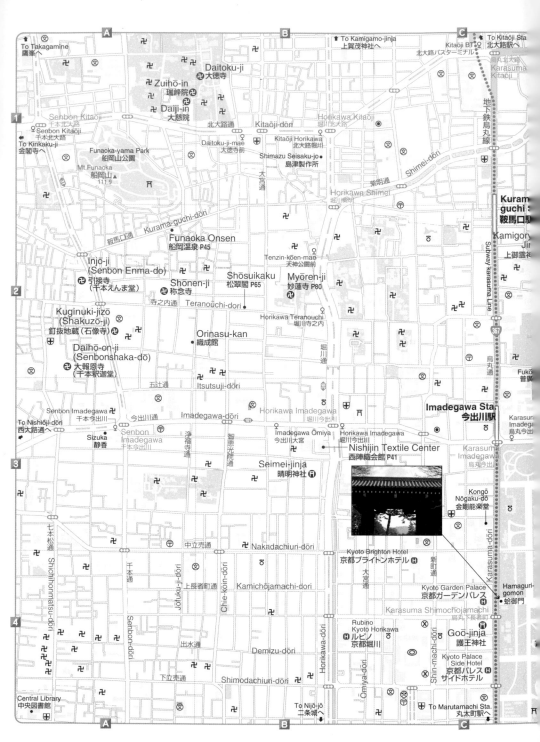

To Takagamine
鷹峯へ

To Kamigamo-jinja
上賀茂神社へ

Kitaōji BT
北大路バスターミナル

To Kitaōji Sta
北大路駅へ

Kitaōji BT
北大路バスターミナル

地下鉄烏丸線

烏丸北大路
Karasuma
Kitaōji

Daitoku-ji
大徳寺

Zuihō-in
瑞峰院

Daiji-in
大慈院

Senbon Kitaōji
千本北大路

To Senbon Kitaōji
千本北大路

To Kinkaku-ji
金閣寺へ

北大路通

Daitoku-ji-mae
大徳寺前

Kitaōji-dōri
北大路通

Kitaōji Horikawa
北大路堀川

Horikawa Kitaōji
堀川北大路

Shimazu Seisaku-jo
島津製作所

Shimei-dōri

Funaoka-yama Park
船岡山公園

Mt.Funaoka
船岡山 ▲
111.9

大宮通

紫明通

Horikawa Shimei
堀川紫明

Subway Karasuma Line

Kuram-
guchi S
鞍馬口駅

Kamigory
Jir
上御霊社

Kurama-guchi-dōri
鞍馬口通

Funaoka Onsen
船岡温泉 P45

Tenzin-kōen-mae
天神公園前

Injō-ji
(Senbon Enma-do)
引接寺
(千本えんま堂)

Shōnen-ji
称念寺

Shōsuikaku
松翠閣 P65

Myōren-ji
妙蓮寺 P80

Teranouchi-dōri
寺之内通

Horikawa Teranouchi
堀川寺之内

Kuginuki-jizō
(Shakuzō-ji)
釘抜地蔵 (石像寺)

Daihō-on-ji
(Senbonshaka-dō)
大報恩寺
(千本釈迦堂)

Orinasu-kan
織成館

堀川通

五辻通

Itsutsuji-dōri
五辻通

Senbon Imadegawa
千本今出川

今出川通

To Nishiōji-dōri
西大路通へ

Sizuka
静香

Senbon
Imadegawa
千本今出川

浄福寺通

智恵光院通

Imadegawa-dōri
今出川通

Horikawa Imadegawa
堀川今出川

Imadegawa Ōmiya
今出川大宮

Horikawa Imadegawa
堀川今出川

Imadegawa Sta
今出川駅

Karasuma
Imadega
烏丸今出

Karasuma
Imadega
烏丸今出

Seimei-jinja
晴明神社

Nishijin Textile Center
西陣織会館 P41

Kongō
Nōgaku-dō
金剛能楽堂

中立売通

Nakadachiuri-dōri

Kyoto Brighton Hotel
京都ブライトンホテル

新町通

Fukō
普賢

367

烏丸通

Shichihonmatsu-dōri
七本松通

千本通

Jōfuku-ji-dōri
上長者町通

Chie-kōin-dōri
智恵光院通

Kamichōjamachi-dori
上長者町通

大宮通

Kyoto Garden Palace
京都ガーデンパレス

Karasuma-dōri

Karasuma Shimochōjamachi
烏丸下長者町

Hamaguri-
gomon
蛤御門

出水通

Demizu-dōri

Horikawa-dōri
堀川通

Rubino
Kyoto Horikawa
ルビノ
京都堀川

Shin-machi-dōri

Goō-jinja
護王神社

Central Library
中央図書館

下立売通

Shimodachiuri-dōri

Senbon-dōri
千本通

Ōmiya-dōri
大宮通

To Nijō-jō
二条城へ

Kyoto Palace
Side Hotel
京都パレス
サイドホテル

To Marutamachi Sta.
丸太町駅へ

To Kitayama-dōri
北山通へ

To Takaragaike
宝ヶ池へ

Shimogamohon-dōri Kitaōji
下鴨本通北大路

• Hōsen
宝泉 P58

To Ichijōji Sta.
一乗寺駅へ

下鴨本通

QANAT Rakuhoku
カナート洛北

Takano
高野

1

Holiday In Kyoto
Hホリデイイン京都

Shimogamo-nishidōri

Shimogamo-
jinja
下鴨神社

To Shirakawa-dōri
白川通へ

Chayama Sta.
茶山駅

Simogamo-jinja
(Kamomioya-jinja)
下鴨神社
(賀茂御祖神社)

Shimogamo-higashi-dōri

叡山電鉄叡山本線

Tadasu-no-mori
糺の森

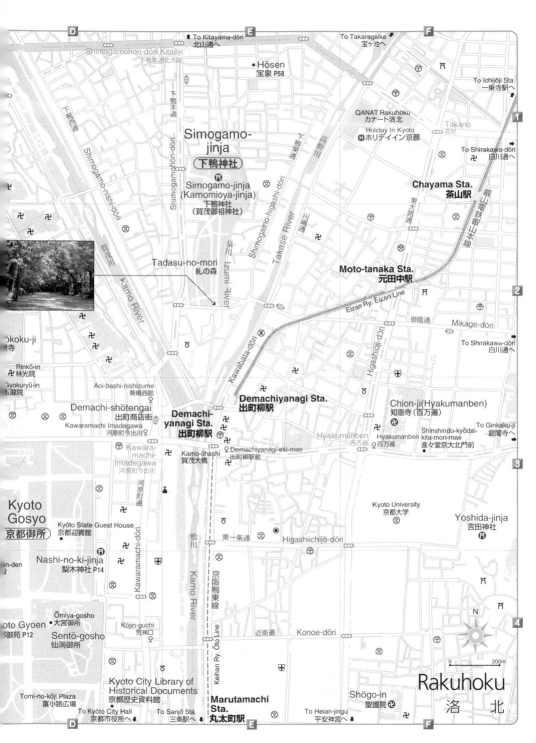

Takase River
Izumi River

Moto-tanaka Sta.
元田中駅

2

Kamo River

Eizan Ry. Eizan Line
叡山電車叡山本線
御蔭通

Mikage-dōri

To Shirakawa-dōri
白川通へ

Kawabata-dōri

Higashiōji-dōri

oku-ji
寺

Rinkō-in
林光院

Byokuryū-in
宝龍院

Aoi-bashi-nishizume
葵橋西詰

Demachiyanagi Sta.
出町柳駅

Chion-ji(Hyakumanben)
知恩寺(百万遍)

Demachi-shōtengai
出町商店街

Demachi-
yanagi Sta.
出町柳駅

To Ginkaku-ji
銀閣寺へ

Kawaramachi Imadegawa
河原町今出川

Hyakumanben
百万遍

Shinshindo-kyōdai-
kita-mon-mae
進々堂京大北門前

Kawara-
machi-
Imadegawa
河原町今出川

Demachiyanagi-eki-mae
出町柳駅前

Kamo-ohashi
賀茂大橋

3

Kyoto
Gosyo
京都御所

Kawaramachi-dōri

河原町通

Kyoto University
京都大学

Yoshida-jinja
吉田神社

Kyōto State Guest House
京都迎賓館

Higashiichijō-dōri
東一条通

Higashiichijō-dōri

Nashi-no-ki-jinja
梨木神社 P14

鴨川

京阪鴨東線

in-den

to Gyoen P12
御苑 P12

Ōmiya-gosho
大宮御所

Kōjin-guchi
荒神口

Konoe-dōri
近衛通

4

Sentō-gosho
仙洞御所

Kamo River

N

Keihan Ry. Ōto Line

0　　200m

Tomi-no-kōji Plaza
富小路広場

Kyoto City Library of
Historical Documents
京都歴史資料館

Rakuhoku

To Kyōto City Hall
京都市役所へ

Marutamachi
Sta.
丸太町駅

Shōgo-in
聖護院

洛 北

To Sanjō Sta.
三条駅へ

To Heian-jingu
平安神宮へ

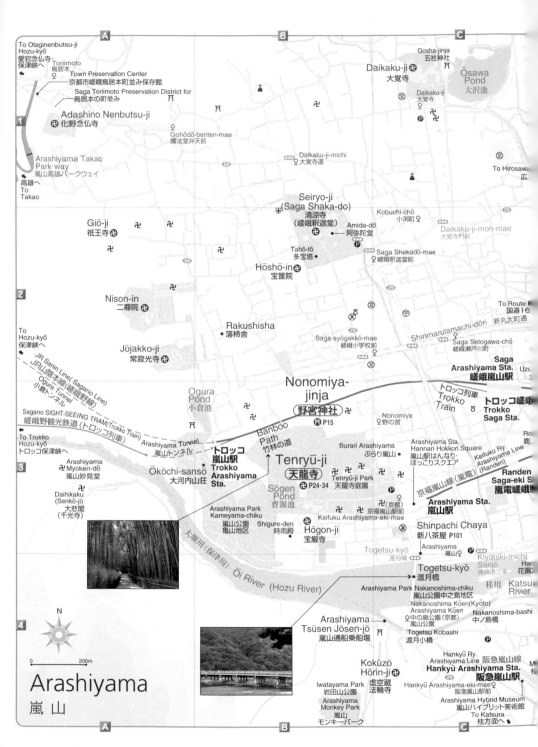

Grid labels

A **B** **C**

1

To Otaginenbutsu-ji
Hozu-kyō
愛宕念仏寺
保津峡へ

Toriimoto
鳥居本

Town Preservation Center
京都市嵯峨鳥居本町並み保存館

Saga Toriimoto Preservation District for
鳥居本の町並み

Adashino Nenbutsu-ji
化野念仏寺

Gohōdō-benten-mae
護法堂弁天前

Arashiyama Takao
Park·way
嵐山高雄パークウェイ
高雄へ
To
Takao

Daikaku-ji
大覚寺

Gosha-jinja
五社神社

Daikaku-ji
大覚寺

Ōsawa
Pond
大沢池

To Hirosawa
広

Daikaku-ji-michi
大覚寺道

Seiryo-ji
(Saga Shaka-do)
清凉寺
(嵯峨釈迦堂)

Kobuchi-chō
小渕町

Amida-dō
阿弥陀堂

Daikaku-ji-mon-mae
大覚寺門前

2

Giō-ji
祇王寺

Tahō-tō
多宝塔

Saga Shakadō-mae
嵯峨釈迦堂前

Hōshō-in
宝筐院

Nison-in
二尊院

Rakushisha
落柿舎

Saga-syōgakkō-mae
嵯峨小学校前

Saga Setogawa-chō
嵯峨瀬戸川町

Shinmarutamachi-dōri
新丸太町通

To Route
国道16
新丸太町通

Saga
Arashiyama-eki
嵯峨嵐山駅

To
Hozu-kyō
保津峡へ

Jōjakko-ji
常寂光寺

Ogura
Pond
小倉池

Nonomiya-
jinja
野宮神社
P15

Uzu

JR Sanin Line(Sagano Line)
JR山陰本線(嵯峨野線)
Ogura Tunnel
小倉トンネル

Sagano SIGHT-SEEING TRAM(Trokko Train)
嵯峨野観光鉄道 (トロッコ列車)

To Trokko
Hozu-kyō
トロッコ保津峡へ

Arashiyama Tunnel
嵐山トンネル

Arashiyama
Myoken-dō
嵐山妙見堂

Daihikaku
(Senkō-ji)
大悲閣
(千光寺)

Ōkōchi-sansō
大河内山荘

3

Trokko
嵐山駅
Trokko
Arashiyama
Sta.

Banboo
Path
竹林の道

Tenryū-ji
天龍寺
P24·34

Nonomiya
野の宮

Burari Arashiyama
ぶらり嵐山

Arashiyama Sta.
Hannari Hokkori Square
嵐山駅はんなり・
ほっこりスクエア

トロッコ列車
Trokko
Train

トロッコ嵯峨
Trokko
Saga Sta.

Keifuku Ry.
Arashiyama Line
(Randen)

Ro
鹿

Randen
Saga-eki S
嵐電嵯峨

京福嵐山線(嵐電)
Keifuku Arashiyama Line(Arashiyama)

Arashiyama Sta.
嵐山駅

Keifuku Arashiyama-eki-mae
京福嵐山駅前

Sōgen
Pond
曹源池

Tenryū-ji Park
天龍寺庭園

Arashiyama Park
Kameyama-chiku
嵐山公園
亀山地区

Shigure-den
時雨殿

Hōgon-ji
宝厳寺

Shinpachi Chaya
新八茶屋 P101

大堰川(保津川) Ōi River (Hozu River)

Togetsu-kyō
渡月橋

Arashiyama
嵐山

Kiyotaki-michi
清滝道三条
Sanjō

Han
花園

Togetsu-kyō
渡月橋

桂川 Katsu
River

4

Arashiyama
Tsūsen Jōsen-jō
嵐山通船乗船場

Arashiyama Park Nakanoshima-chiku
嵐山公園中之島地区

Nakanoshima Kōen(Kyōto)
中ノ島公園(京都)
Arashiyama Kōen
嵐山公園

Togetsu Kobashi
渡月小橋

Nakanoshima-bashi
中ノ島橋

N

0   200m

Arashiyama
嵐山

Iwatayama Park
岩田山公園

Arashiyama
Monkey Park
嵐山
モンキーパーク

Kokūzō
Hōrin-ji
虚空蔵
法輪寺

Hankyū Ry.
Arashiyama Line 阪急嵐山線
Hankyū Arashiyama Sta.
阪急嵐山駅

Hankyū Arashiyama-eki-mae
阪急嵐山駅前

Arashiyama Hybrid Museum
嵐山ハイブリット美術館
To Katsura
桂方面へ

M

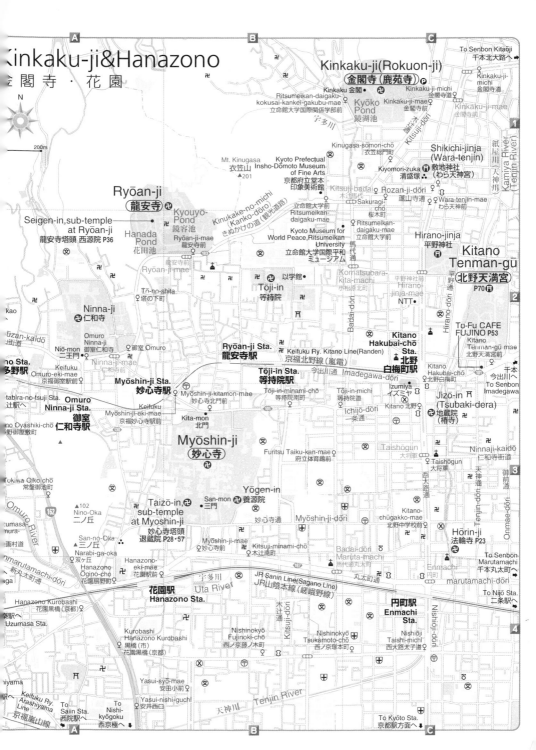

Kinkaku-ji&Hanazono
金閣寺・花園

Kinkaku-ji(Rokuon-ji)
金閣寺(鹿苑寺)

N

200m

Kinkaku-ji-michi
金閣寺道

Kinkaku-ji-mae
金閣寺前

To Senbon Kitaōji
千本北大路へ

Kinkaku 金閣

Ritsumeikan-daigaku-kokusai-kankei-gakubu-mae
立命館大学国際関係学部前

Kyōko Pond
鏡湖池

Kinkaku-ji-mae
金閣寺前

Shikichi-jinja
(Wara-tenjin)
敷地神社
(わら天宮)

Mt. Kinugasa
衣笠山
▲201

Kyoto Prefectural
Insho-Dōmoto Museum of Fine Arts
京都府立堂本印象美術館

Kinugasa-sōmon-chō
衣笠総門町

Kiyomori-zuka
清盛塚

Rozan-ji-chō
蘆山寺通

Wara-tenjin-mae
わら天神前

Ryōan-ji
龍安寺

Seigen-in,sub-temple at Ryōan-ji
龍安寺塔頭 西源院 P36

Kyouyō-Pond
鏡容池

Kinukake-no-michi
(Kanko-dōri)
きぬかけの道(観光道路)

Ryōan-ji-mae
龍安寺前

Sakuragi-chō
桜木町

Ritsumeikan-daigaku-mae
立命館大学前

Kyoto Museum for World Peace,Ritsumeikan University
立命館大学国際平和ミュージアム

Hirano-jinja
平野神社

Kitano Tenman-gū
北野天満宮
P70

Hanada Pond
花田池

Ryōan-ji-mae
龍安寺前

Tō-no-shita
塔の下町

Tōji-in
等持院

以学館

Komatsubara-kita-machi
小松原北町

Hirano-jinja-mae
平野神社前

NTT

Hirano-dōri
平野通

Tō-Fu CAFE FUJINO P53

Ninna-ji
仁和寺

Nio-mon
二王門

Omuro Ninna-ji
御室 仁和寺

Omuro Omuro
御室 Omuro

Kitano Hakubai-chō Sta.
北野白梅町駅

Keifuku Ry. Kitano Line(Randen)
京福北野線(嵐電)

Kitano Tenman-gū mae
北野天満宮前

Kitano Hakubai-chō
北野白梅町

To Senbon Imadegawa
千本今出川へ

Ryōan-ji Sta.
龍安寺駅

Imadegawa-dōri
今出川通 Imadegawa-dōri

Izumiya
イズミヤ

Kitano 北野

Myoshin-ji Sta.
妙心寺駅

Tōji-in Sta.
等持院駅

Tōji-in-minami-chō
等持院南町

Tōji-in-michi
等持院通

Ichijō-dōri
一条通

Jizō-in
(Tsubaki-dera)
地蔵院
(椿寺)

Keifuku Omuro-eki-mae
京福御室駅前

Keifuku Myōshin-ji Sta.
京福妙心寺駅前

Kita-mon
北門

Myōshin-ji-kitamon-mae
妙心寺北門前

Omuro Ninna-ji Sta.
御室 仁和寺駅

Oyashiki-chō
御屋敷町

Taishōgun
大将軍

Furitsu Taiku-kan-mae
府立体育館前

Taishōgun
大将軍

Ninnaji-kaidō
仁和寺街道

Myōshin-ji
妙心寺

Kita-mon
北門

Nino-Oka
二ノ丘 ▲102

San-no-Oka
三ノ丘

Narabi-ga-oka
双ヶ丘

Taizō-in, sub-temple at Myoshin-ji
妙心寺塔頭 退蔵院 P28・57

San-mon
三門

Yōgen-in
養源院

Myōshin-ji-dōri
妙心寺通

Kitano-chūgakko-mae
北野中学校前

Hōrin-ji
法輪寺 P23

To Senbon Marutamachi
千本丸太町へ

Hanazono-eki-mae
花園駅前

Hanazono Ogino-chō
花園荻野町

Myōshin-ji-mae
妙心寺前

Kitsuji-minami-chō
木辻南町

Badai-dōri
馬代通

Maruta-machi
丸太町

Enmachi
円町

Marutamachi-dōri
marutamachi-dōri

Omuro River
御室川

San-no-Oka
三ノ丘

Hanazono Sta.
花園駅

JR Sanin Line(Sagano Line)
JR山陰本線(嵯峨野線)

Uta River
宇多川 Uta River

To Nijō Sta.
二条駅へ

Enmachi Sta.
円町駅

Kurobashi Hanazono Kurobashi
黒橋(市)
花園黒橋(京都)

Nishinokyō Fujinoki-chō
西ノ京藤ノ木町

Nishinokyō Tsukamoto-chō
西ノ京塚本町

Nishiōji Taishi-michi
西大路太子道

Nishiōji-dōri
西大路通

Kitsuji-dōri
木辻通

To Kyōto Sta.
京都駅方面へ

Yasui-syō-mae
安田小前

Yasui-nishi-guchi
安田西口

Tenjin River
天神川 Tenjin River

Keifuku Ry. Arashiyama-sen
京福嵐山線

To Saiin Sta.
西院駅へ

To Nishi-kyōgoku
西京極へ

KYOTO The Greatest Travel Tips
英語で歩く京都

2008年3月15日初版印刷
2008年4月1日初版発行

編集人…阿部由美子
発行人…江頭　誠

発行所…
JTBパブリッシング
〒162-8446　東京都新宿区払方町25-5　アーバンネット市ヶ谷ビル

編集・制作…
JTBパブリッシング関西編集部
〒530-0002　大阪市北区曽根崎新地2-2-16　桜橋東洋ビル3階
06-6345-1011（編集）　03-6888-7893（販売）

編集・取材スタッフ…
のぞみ（岡本亜美、奥茉莉子、冬木明里、堀池涼子）
勇上香織、坂永紀江

表紙デザイン…扇谷デザイン事務所（扇谷正昭）
デザイン…エスティフ
イラスト…いぬんこ
写真協力…大島拓也
撮影協力…宍戸大全アクション軍団
翻訳協力…翻訳センター
地図…ジェイマップ、データアトラス、NDS

組　版　エスティフ
印刷所　JTB印刷

この本に掲載した記事やデータは、2008年1月31日現在のものです。
発行後に、料金、営業時間、定休日、メニュー等の営業内容が変更になることや、臨時
休業等で利用できない場合があります。
また、各種データを含めた掲載内容の正確性には万全を期しておりますが、おでかけの際
には電話等で事前に確認・予約されることをお勧めいたします。
なお、本書に掲載された内容による損害等は、弊社では補償いたしかねますので、予めご
了承くださいますようお願いいたします。

All information on this book is based on data as of Jan.31, 2008.
Information about charges, business hours, regular holidays, and menus could be changed.
And shops could have an extra holiday.
While every effort is made to ensure the accuracy of all information, you should confirm open-
ing hours, or make a reservation by the telephone before your visit.
Your use of this book is at your own risk. Our company is not liable for any losses or troubles.

※本書掲載の地図は国土地理院発行の50万分の1地方図、20万分の1地勢図、5万
分の1地形図、数値地図25000（空間データ基盤）を調整したものです。（承認番号平
18総使、第78-830号／平18総使、第79-830号／平18総使、第80-830号／平18総
使、第81-830号）※本誌掲載のレリーフマップは、「カシミール3D」を使用し、作成しました。

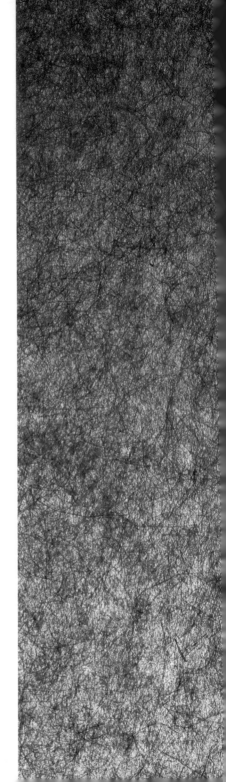